# THEY PLAYED

## Baseball

### FOR THE

# Giants?

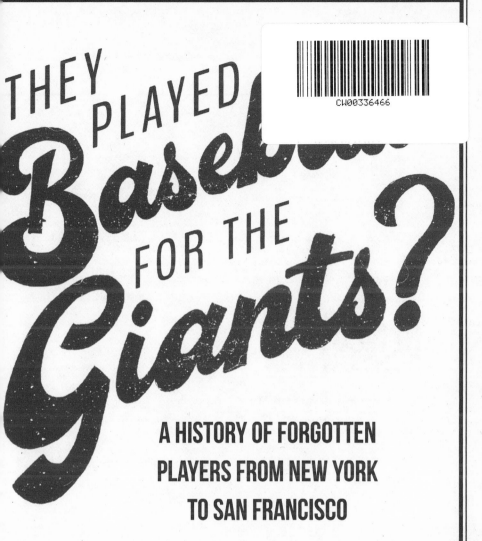

## A HISTORY OF FORGOTTEN
## PLAYERS FROM NEW YORK
## TO SAN FRANCISCO

# JEFF
# WAGNER

**www.mascotbooks.com**

*They Played Baseball for the Giants?*

©2020 Jeff Wagner. All Rights Reserved. No part of this publication may
be reproduced, stored in a retrieval system or transmitted in any form by
any means electronic, mechanical, or photocopying, recording or otherwise
without the permission of the author.

**For more information, please contact:**
Mascot Books
620 Herndon Parkway #320
Herndon, VA 20170
info@mascotbooks.com

Library of Congress Control Number: 2019914050

CPSIA Code: PRFRE0120A
ISBN-13: 978-1-64543-157-2

Printed in Canada

This book is dedicated to the memory of my father, Jim Wagner, who took me to my first professional basketball game in 1966, my first professional hockey game in 1969, my first professional baseball game in 1971, and my first professional football game in 1975. He not only introduced me to the world of sports, but instilled the importance of good sportsmanship and team work whenever playing one.

Also to the memory of my sister Julie Martinez, who was probably a bigger Bay Area sports fan than I was. She would have loved this book!

And last but not least, I would also like to thank my loving wife Amy for her support, even though she has little to no interest in baseball. Thanks for the encouragement!

# CONTENTS

## THE END OF THE LINE                                    37

## OTHER PLAYERS OF NOTE                                  53
## THE GIANTS BY THE NUMBERS                              54
## THE GIANTS - A TIMELINE                                56
## SOURCES                                                64
## ABOUT THE AUTHOR                                       65

# INTRODUCTION

The Giants have had a large and storied role in the history of Major League Baseball. Going back to its roots in New York as the Gothams in 1883 and Giants in 1885, to their moving to San Francisco in 1958, the Giants have won more games than any other franchise in Major League baseball history (11,088) as of 2019. They were also the first franchise to reach the 10,000 and 11,000 win plateau. Their .536 winning percentage is only second to the Yankees (.569) in baseball history. And surprising to many, they have more Hall-of-Famers than any other team with 57.

## THE GIANTS IN HISTORY

| | |
|---|---|
| **TEAM NAMES:** | SAN FRANCISCO GIANTS, NEW YORK GIANTS, NEW YORK GOTHAMS |
| **SEASONS:** | 137 (1883 to 2019) |
| **RECORD:** | 11,105 - 9,625 (.536 W-L%) |
| **PLAYOFF APPEARANCES:** | 26 |
| **PENNANTS:** | 23 |
| **WORLD CHAMPIONSHIPS:** | 8 |
| **WINNINGEST MANAGER:** | JOHN McGRAW, 2583-1790 (591 W-L %) |

Everyone knows of the greats who have had long careers with the Giants: Hall of Famers Christy Mathewson, Mel Ott, Carl Hubbell, Bill Terry, Willie Mays, Willie McCovey and Juan Marichal; as well as Barry Bonds, Will Clark, Tim Lincecum, and Buster Posey to name just a few.

But did you know that at one time or another, 15 other Hall of Famers have made stops in either New York or San Francisco? Not to mention two NFL Hall of Famers, an Olympic champion, and a character from a popular movie? So I hope you'll enjoy discovering the interesting stories surrounding how and why these, and over 35 other players you may have forgotten about or maybe even didn't know about, spent time in a Giants uniform, and what they did while they were one.

You'll find player stories broken up chronologically in three categories based on their time with the Giants:

1. *"The Start of Something Big"*: players who began their career as a Giant but spent most of their playing days elsewhere.
2. *"Hello and Goodbye"*: players who had short tenures as a Giant during their career.
3. *"The End of the Line"*: players who flourished with other teams but retired as a Giant.

# THE START OF SOMETHING BIG

After observing the nine players that make up this category, players who started their careers as a Giant, you'll notice one other thing that most have in common: they had great careers once they left. And in many cases, you'll also note that the trades that involved these players didn't exactly work out for the best. But these, of course, only represent a small portion of the trades made by Giant management throughout history. Just as many have been made that wound up working out very well for the team.

So although these players were all rookies with the Giants, they weren't around long enough, or didn't do much when they were there, for many people to remember.

- Archibald Graham
- Willie Keeler
- Frankie Frisch
- Hack Wilson
- Hoyt Wilhelm
- George Foster
- Dave Kingman
- Garry Maddox
- Gary Matthews

# ARCHIBALD GRAHAM

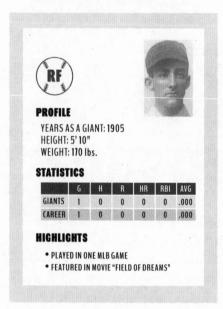

**PROFILE**
YEARS AS A GIANT: 1905
HEIGHT: 5' 10"
WEIGHT: 170 lbs.

**STATISTICS**

|  | G | H | R | HR | RBI | AVG |
|---|---|---|---|---|---|---|
| GIANTS | 1 | 0 | 0 | 0 | 0 | .000 |
| CAREER | 1 | 0 | 0 | 0 | 0 | .000 |

**HIGHLIGHTS**

- PLAYED IN ONE MLB GAME
- FEATURED IN MOVIE "FIELD OF DREAMS"

Archibald "Moonlight" Graham. If you're a fan of baseball movies, that name should sound very familiar to you. In the 1989 movie *"Field of Dreams,"* Graham was the player who saved Kevin Costner's choking daughter after his one and only Major League at-bat. Graham had just fulfilled his dream of facing a major league pitcher before crossing back into the present day to fulfill his duty as a doctor. If this sounds confusing, then you'll have to watch the movie!

Interestingly, Graham was a real person who actually did only play in one Major League baseball game, and that was with the New York Giants. On June 29, 1905 at Washington Park, Graham replaced outfielder George Browne in the bottom of the eighth inning. In the top of the ninth, Graham was on deck when the last out of the inning was made. So although in actuality he never did get a Major League at bat, the movie-makers did the next best thing: they gave him another chance. And in the movie, Graham hit a sacrifice fly to right field, driving in a run. Regardless, he was ultimately credited with playing in one Major League game. Graham spent the rest of the season, and his career, in the minor leagues before quitting baseball after the 1908 season. On a side note, Graham was a lefty, hitting and throwing from the left side. He was portrayed as a righty in the movie.

One thing the movie did portray accurately was that Graham was a doctor. "Doc" Graham obtained his medical degree from the University of Maryland in 1905, and after he retired practiced medicine in Chisholm, Minnesota, serving the people there for 50 years. He died in Chisholm in 1965 at the age of 88.

# WILLIE KEELER

"Wee" Willie Keeler, all 5'4", 140 pounds of him, played 18 years in the Major Leagues, and has the distinction of being the only player on this list who both began (1892) and ended (1910) his career as a Giant. Unfortunately for the Giants, it was the 16 years in between where he left his mark in baseball history. After a lackluster first season where he only played in 14 games, the Giants sold Keeler to Brooklyn 20 games into his second season for $800.

During his time with Brooklyn, Baltimore and the New York Yankees, Keeler's uncanny ability to bunt is credited as the reason a specific rule was added to

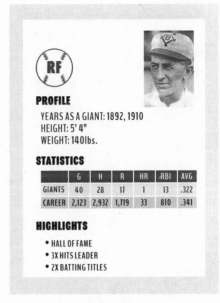

**RF**

**PROFILE**
YEARS AS A GIANT: 1892, 1910
HEIGHT: 5' 4"
WEIGHT: 140 lbs.

**STATISTICS**

|        | G     | H     | R     | HR | RBI | AVG  |
|--------|-------|-------|-------|-----|-----|------|
| GIANTS | 40    | 28    | 17    | 1   | 13  | .322 |
| CAREER | 2,123 | 2,932 | 1,719 | 33  | 810 | .341 |

**HIGHLIGHTS**
- HALL OF FAME
- 3X HITS LEADER
- 2X BATTING TITLES

the Major League Baseball rule book. Because of his bunting ability, Keeler was able to bunt most balls pitched to him, enabling him to avoid striking out. In in the 1899 season, Keeler struck out only twice in 570 at bats, still an at-bat-per-strikeout ratio Major League Baseball record, and one that is safe to say will never be broken. His unique skill at prolonging at bats by continually fouling pitches off was the stimulus for the rule change that made a foul bunt with two strikes a strikeout.

In 1897, Keeler had a 44-game hitting streak to start the season and a hit in his final game of the 1896 season, giving him a National League-record 45-game hitting streak. This mark was surpassed by Joe DiMaggio's 56-game hitting streak in 1941 and matched in 1978 by Pete Rose. Keeler also had eight consecutive seasons with 200 or more hits, a record that lasted until 2009 when Ichiro Suzuki had his ninth consecutive 200 hit season. Ichiro added a 10th consecutive season in 2010.

When he signed as a free agent with the Giants on May 6, 1910, Keeler returned to play one final season with the team he started with some 18 years earlier. Keeler wound up only playing in 19 games in 2010, getting three hits and three walks in his final 10 at bats as a major leaguer. Still, the right fielder's .341 lifetime batting average, 2,932 hits and two batting titles were enough to earn him a place in baseball's Hall of Fame. He retired at the age of 38.

# FRANKIE FRISCH

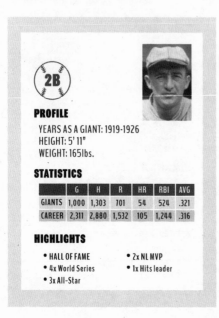

**PROFILE**
YEARS AS A GIANT: 1919-1926
HEIGHT: 5' 11"
WEIGHT: 165lbs.

**STATISTICS**

|  | G | H | R | HR | RBI | AVG |
|---|---|---|---|---|---|---|
| GIANTS | 1,000 | 1,303 | 701 | 54 | 524 | .321 |
| CAREER | 2,311 | 2,880 | 1,532 | 105 | 1,244 | .316 |

**HIGHLIGHTS**

- HALL OF FAME
- 4x World Series
- 3x All-Star
- 2x NL MVP
- 1x Hits leader

Widely regarded as one of the greatest second basemen in Major League baseball history, Frankie Frisch's career really began to take off in his third season as a Giant in 1921 when he knocked out 211 hits for a .341 average with eight home runs and an even 100 RBIs. He also had a career high 49 stolen bases, which led the league. Two years later he had a career high .348 average and career and league high 223 hits.

History has it that after an August 1926 loss in which Frisch had missed a sign, costing the Giants a run, Manager John McGraw loudly berated Frisch in front of the team. Frisch responded by leaving the team, and with his previously close relationship with McGraw virtually ended, the club decided to trade their 28-year-old All-Star (plus pitcher Jimmy Ring) to the St. Louis Cardinals for the only other 2nd baseman regarded better than he…Rogers Hornsby. Hornsby was coming off a subpar 1925 season where he "only" hit .317. But following consecutive seasons of .370, .397, .401, .384, .424 and .403 batting averages, each leading the National League, and at 31 years of age, the Cardinals decided to trade for a younger Frisch after contract negotiations with Hornsby fell apart.

Frisch went on to have 11 productive seasons with the Cardinals, including 1931 where he won the league MVP, and 1927 when he finished 2nd. As leader of their "Gashouse Gang", Frisch played in three All-Star games with the Cardinals. In total, Frisch appeared in seven World Series, winning four of them (two with Giants, two with Cardinals). Hornsby, on the other hand, only stuck around with the Giants for one year (see his write up under "*Hello and Goodbye*"),

Frisch was also a player/manager for the Cardinals from 1933-1937. After managing them one more season, Frisch moved on to helm the Pittsburgh Pirates from 1940-1946 and the Chicago Cubs from 1949-1951. His record in his 16 year managerial career was 1,138-1078.

Despite all of his success with the Cardinals, Frank Frisch will always go down as a rookie with the New York Giants.

# HACK WILSON

Unfortunately, the Frank Frisch trade wouldn't be the only questionable one the Giants would make during this time period. In 1925, after three lackluster seasons as a New York Giant, including his best in 1924 when he hit .295 with 10 home runs and 57 RBIs in only 107 games, the Giants dealt Hack Wilson, a husky 5'6", 190 lb, 25-year-old outfielder to the Chicago Cubs for right fielder Earl Webb. Webb played in four games for the Giants in 1925 and went hitless in three at bats. In late 1925, Webb was ironically traded back to the Cubs for Ty Tyson. Tyson, also an outfielder, spent the next two seasons with the Giants, playing in 140 games with four home runs, 52 RBIs and a decent .283 average.

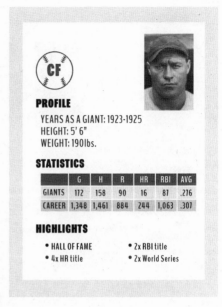

**PROFILE**
YEARS AS A GIANT: 1923-1925
HEIGHT: 5' 6"
WEIGHT: 190 lbs.

**STATISTICS**

|  | G | H | R | HR | RBI | AVG |
|---|---|---|---|---|---|---|
| GIANTS | 112 | 158 | 90 | 16 | 87 | .276 |
| CAREER | 1,348 | 1,461 | 884 | 244 | 1,063 | .307 |

**HIGHLIGHTS**
- HALL OF FAME
- 4x HR title
- 2x RBI title
- 2x World Series

Wilson, on the other hand, spent the next six seasons with the Cubs, hitting .322 with 190 home runs and 769 RBIs. He led the National League in home runs in his first season with the Cubs (1926), as well as in 1927, 1928 and 1930. In 1930, Wilson had his best season by far when he knocked out 56 home runs, a still all-time record 191 RBIs, and a .356 batting average. Wilson went on to play three seasons with the Brooklyn Dodgers (1932-34) before retiring with the Philadelphia Phillies a year later. But like Frisch, Wilson will go down as a rookie for the New York Giants.

# HOYT WILHELM

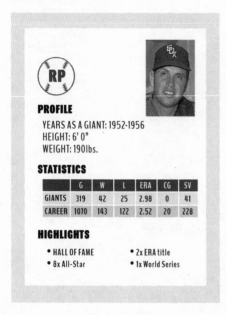

**PROFILE**
YEARS AS A GIANT: 1952-1956
HEIGHT: 6' 0"
WEIGHT: 190lbs.

**STATISTICS**

|  | G | W | L | ERA | CG | SV |
|---|---|---|---|---|---|---|
| GIANTS | 319 | 42 | 25 | 2.98 | 0 | 41 |
| CAREER | 1070 | 143 | 122 | 2.52 | 20 | 228 |

**HIGHLIGHTS**

- HALL OF FAME
- 8x All-Star
- 2x ERA title
- 1x World Series

It's not every day you when you come across a 29-year-old rookie who ended up playing 21 years in the Major Leagues. But that's just what knuckleball specialist Hoyt Wilhelm did. In 1952, Wilhelm, a converted starter who pitched mainly in relief, launched his long career as a member of the New York Giants, where he amazingly won 15 games without starting any of them. He also captured the National League ERA title that year with a 2.43 mark. Two years later, Wilhelm went 12-4 with an ERA of 2.10, again without starting any of the games. In fact, he wouldn't start his first game until 1958 as a member of the Cleveland Indians.

In his third game as a Giant, Wilhelm batted for the first time and hit a home run over the right-field fence at the Polo Grounds. Although he went on to bat another 431 times in his career, that would be his only one.

On February 26, 1957, Wilhelm was traded by the Giants to the St. Louis Cardinals for Whitey Lockman. After earning 11 saves with a 1–4 record and a then career high 4.25 ERA, the Cardinals placed Wilhelm on waivers that September. After being picked up by the Cleveland Indians, Wilhelm started six of 30 games for the tribe in 1958 before being released and claimed by the Baltimore Orioles on August 23rd. Five weeks later, he would no-hit the eventual World Champion New York Yankees 1-0 at Memorial Stadium in only his ninth career start.

Wilhelm pitched until 1972 when, just 16 days short of his 50th birthday, he was released by the Los Angeles Dodgers on July 21 after appearing in 16 games and registering a 4.62 ERA over 25 innings. Wilhelm would soon retire. At the time of his retirement, Wilhelm had pitched in a then major league record 1,070 games, starting 52 of them. He is recognized as the first pitcher to have saved 200 games in his career, and the first pitcher to appear in 1,000 games. He also still holds the Major League record of 124 wins in relief. He would be the first relief pitcher to enter the Hall-of-Fame in 1985.

# GEORGE FOSTER

When you hear the name "George Foster," most people think of the Big Red Machine of the 1970's. Johnny Bench, Pete Rose, Joe Morgan…and George Foster. Foster was the slugger who drove in Rose, Morgan and Ken Griffey, thanks, in part, by having Bench hitting behind him.

But before all of that, however, Foster spent his first two seasons as a San Francisco Giant, occasionally playing in the same outfield as Willie Mays and Bobby Bonds. Foster played in 54 total games for the Giants, knocking out 36 hits in 129 plate appearances, including four home runs, 13 RBIs and a .279 batting average. In May 1971, Foster was traded to the

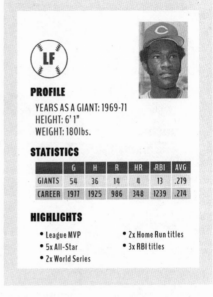

**PROFILE**
YEARS AS A GIANT: 1969-71
HEIGHT: 6' 1"
WEIGHT: 180lbs.

**STATISTICS**

|        | G    | H    | R   | HR  | RBI  | AVG  |
|--------|------|------|-----|-----|------|------|
| GIANTS | 54   | 36   | 14  | 4   | 13   | .279 |
| CAREER | 1977 | 1925 | 986 | 348 | 1239 | .274 |

**HIGHLIGHTS**
- League MVP
- 5x All-Star
- 2x World Series
- 2x Home Run titles
- 3x RBI titles

Cincinnati Reds for light hitting infielder Frank Duffy and hurler Vern Geishert, who never pitched a game for the Giants. Duffy played in 21 games with San Francisco and batted .179 in 28 at bats before being traded with Gaylord Perry to the Cleveland Indians for Sam McDowell shortly after the 1971 season. You can read more about McDowell under *"Hello and Goodbye"*.

Foster, on the other hand, played in 104 games for the Reds in 1971, smacking 10 home runs and 50 RBIs while batting .234. After a mediocre 1972 and 1974 seasons surrounding an injury-filled 1973 season, things finally started to click for Foster in 1975 when he batted .305 with 23 homers and 78 RBIs. Two years later he would win the National League MVP when he knocked out league leading 52 home runs and 149 RBIs while hitting .320. Foster wound up playing 16 years after leaving the Giants, including 11 with the Reds, five with the Mets, and two games with the White Sox, belting out a career total 348 homers, 1,239 RBIs and a .274 average.

Makes you wonder what it was that the Reds saw in Foster that the Giants didn't. Unlike the Giants, though, their patience paid off.

# DAVE KINGMAN

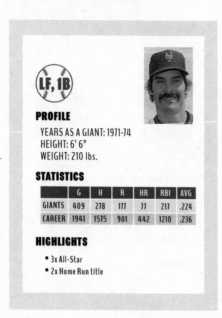

**LF, 1B**

**PROFILE**
YEARS AS A GIANT: 1971-74
HEIGHT: 6' 6"
WEIGHT: 210 lbs.

**STATISTICS**

|  | G | H | R | HR | RBI | AVG |
|---|---|---|---|---|---|---|
| GIANTS | 409 | 278 | 177 | 77 | 217 | .224 |
| CAREER | 1941 | 1575 | 901 | 442 | 1210 | .236 |

**HIGHLIGHTS**

• 3x All-Star
• 2x Home Run title

Dave "King Kong" Kingman was drafted out of high school in 1967 by the California Angels and in 1968 by the Baltimore Orioles, but chose, instead, to attend the University of Southern California to play college baseball for the USC Trojans as a pitcher. Yes, you heard that right: a pitcher. And not a bad one at that, as in 1969 he finished with an 11–4 record with a 1.38 ERA. He also hit .250 with four home runs and 16 RBIs as a part-time hitter for the Trojans.

Following winning the 1970 USC NCAA Championship Season and being named an All-American that year, the Giants drafted Kingman with the first pick of the 1970 secondary phase draft, with the intention of playing him in the field. Kingman made his major league debut on July 30, 1971, pinch running for Willie McCovey, and finishing the game at first base. He hit a home run in his next game, a grand slam, and hit two more a day later.

On the second day of the 1972 season, Kingman hit for the cycle in a Giants' 10–6 victory over the Houston Astros. "Kong" would go on to hit 29 and 24 home runs in his second and third seasons in San Francisco, but only batted.225 and .203. The primary reason for the discrepancy was something that would prove to be a nemesis for Kingman during his entire career: the strikeout. When he retired after the 1986 season, Kingman would be the fourth All-Time leader in strikeouts.

In 1974, Kingman's home run total dropped to 18 with 125 strikeouts in 121 games while he continued to bat in the .220's. After the season, the Giants sold the rights to Kingman to the New York Mets for $150,000. "Kong" would hit 36 and 37 homers the next two seasons for the Mets.

Kingman would play for five more teams in his 16-year career, hitting 442 home runs, 1,210 RBIs, while posting a .235 career average. He won home run titles in 1979 (48) and 1982 (37). He went out with a bang in his final season in 1986, belting 35 home runs and driving in 94 for the Oakland A's.

In four seasons and 409 games with the Giants, Kingman hit .224 with 77 home runs and 217 RBI.

# GARRY MADDOX

Garry Maddox's story was in a way oppo-site of Foster's. Maddox showed some promise right out of the gate, knocking out 12 homers and 58 RBIs his rookie season in 1972. He followed that up with a superb 1973 where he whacked 11 homers, 76 RBIs and hit .319. Although he hit .284 his third season, his produc-tivity dropped to eight home runs and 50 RBIs. And after a slow start in 1975 where he only hit .179 after 17 games, the Giants decided to trade Maddox to the Philadelphia Phillies for Willie Montanez, a player in somewhat the same boat with the Phillies. After finishing 2nd in Rookie of the Year honors in 1971 where he

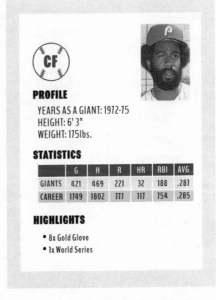

**PROFILE**
YEARS AS A GIANT: 1972-75
HEIGHT: 6' 3"
WEIGHT: 175lbs.

**STATISTICS**

|  | G | H | R | HR | RBI | AVG |
|---|---|---|---|---|---|---|
| GIANTS | 421 | 469 | 221 | 32 | 188 | .281 |
| CAREER | 1749 | 1802 | 777 | 117 | 754 | .285 |

**HIGHLIGHTS**
- 8x Gold Glove
- 1x World Series

clubbed 30 home runs and drove in 99 runs, Montanez followed up his hot start with three sub-par seasons, and the Phillies were ready for a change as well.

After the trade, Maddox hit .291 with four homers and 46 RBIs in 1975 and went on to put together a solid 12 year career with the Phillies, winning eight gold gloves and one World Series. Montanez finished 1975 hitting a superb .305 for the Giants with eight home runs and 85 RBIs. In 1976, after playing 60 games and hitting .309, the Giants shipped Montanez to the Atlanta Braves with three other players for third baseman Darrell Evans and infielder Marty Perez. Perez finished the year before being traded to the Yankees in 1977 for Terry Whitfield, which ended up being a nice trade for the Giants. Whitfield had four strong seasons with San Francisco, while Evans became a fan favorite for the Giants and an All-Star during the next seven seasons.

So after all was said and done, the Giants had technically traded Garry Maddox for Darryl Evans and Terry Whitfield. Not too bad actually when you look back at it now.

# GARY MATTHEWS

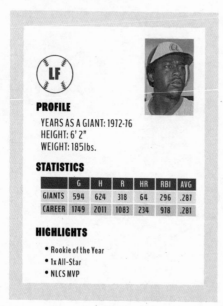

Gary Matthews, like teammate Maddox, started out strong with solid seasons from 1973-76, including winning Rookie of the Year honors in 1973 when he hit .300. In 1976, 25-year-old Matthews continued his production with a solid .284, 20 home run and 84 RBI season. On November 4, 1976, however, a new thing called free agency went into effect. Matthews, deciding to take advantage of it, signed a lucrative $240,000 a year deal with the Atlanta Braves on November 17, up from the $36,000 he was making as a Giant.

Matthews went on to play four years with the Braves, three years with the Phillies, and three years with the Cubs before retiring as a Seattle Mariner in 1987, 16 years after starting his career with the Giants. Oddly enough, he played more games as a Giant (594) than with any other team, but he's probably best known for his time with the Phillies where he was the 1983 World Series MVP.

# HELLO AND GOODBYE

These well-known names were technically Giants, but were only around for a handshake and a quick cup of coffee. None began or ended their careers as a Giant, and some were around for only part of a season. Nevertheless, these 23 big name players will always be members of the Giants family.

- Jim Thorpe
- Casey Stengel
- Rogers Hornsby
- Johnny Mize
- Joe Medwick
- Eddie Stanky
- Harvey Kuenn
- Ed Bailey
- Sam McDowell
- Bobby Mercer
- Joe Morgan
- Al Oliver
- Manny Trillo
- Steve Carlton
- Rich Gossage
- Gary Carter
- Darryl Strawberry
- Deion Sanders
- Orel Hershiser
- Andres Galarraga
- Omar Vizquel
- Miguel Tejada
- Carlos Beltran

# JIM THORPE

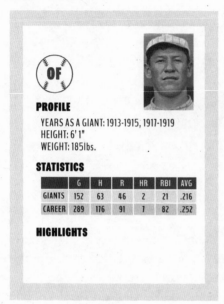

**OF**

**PROFILE**
YEARS AS A GIANT: 1913-1915, 1917-1919
HEIGHT: 6'1"
WEIGHT: 185lbs.

**STATISTICS**

|  | G | H | R | HR | RBI | AVG |
|---|---|---|---|---|---|---|
| GIANTS | 152 | 63 | 46 | 2 | 21 | .216 |
| CAREER | 289 | 176 | 91 | 7 | 82 | .252 |

**HIGHLIGHTS**

Before you ask, yes, this is the same Jim Thorpe who won Pentathlon and Decathlon Gold Medals in the 1912 Olympics and played in the NFL from 1920-1928. Thorpe was a member of the inaugural NFL Hall-of-Fame class in 1963, 10 years after his death.

As far as his baseball career, Thorpe signed with the Giants in 1913 and played sporadically with them through 1915. After a stint in the minor leagues in 1916, Thorpe returned to the Giants in 1917 but was sold to the Cincinnati Reds early in the season. Later that year however, he was sold back to the Giants. He again played sparingly with them through 1918 before being traded to the Boston Braves on May 21, 1919 for Pat Ragan. During his time with the Giants, Thorpe played in 152 games, hitting two home runs, driving in 21 runs and hitting .216.

In his six-year Major League Baseball career, Thorpe played in 289 games, amassed 176 hits for a .252 career average. He parked seven home runs, drove in 82 runs and stole 29 of 32 bases. He retired from baseball for good in 1922 to concentrate on his football career.

# CASEY STENGEL

On the surface, Casey Stengel's three year stay with the New York Giants during his 14-year playing career was nothing to brag about. Primarily used as a pinch hitter and occasional starter, Stengel only played in 177 games during that span. However, something else was happening to him during that time that would eventually propel Stengel into the arena in which he was best known for: managing. While sitting on the bench during that three-year period, Stengel was learning from, and being groomed by, a legend...Giants iconic manager John McGraw.

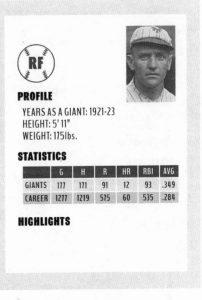

**PROFILE**
YEARS AS A GIANT: 1921-23
HEIGHT: 5'11"
WEIGHT: 175lbs.

**STATISTICS**

| | G | H | R | HR | RBI | AVG |
|---|---|---|---|---|---|---|
| GIANTS | 177 | 111 | 91 | 12 | 93 | .349 |
| CAREER | 1277 | 1219 | 575 | 60 | 535 | .284 |

**HIGHLIGHTS**

Nine years after retiring from playing, Stengel began his storied managerial career with the Brooklyn Dodgers (1934-36) and the Boston Bees/Braves (1938-1943). But it wasn't until six years late when Stengel's legacy really began.

Starting in 1949, Stengel managed the New York Yankees for the next 11 years, winning 10 pennants and seven World Series, including a record five in a row from 1949–1953. In 1960, Stengel hopped across town to manage the expansion New York Mets for three years before retiring in 1965. Stengel is also the only man to have worn the uniform of all four Major League Baseball teams in New York City in the 20th century: the Dodgers, Giants, Yankees and Mets.

As a Giants player, Stengel did post an impressive batting average of .349 in the 177 games he played in. He clubbed 12 home runs and drove in 93 runs in his three years.

# ROGERS HORNSBY

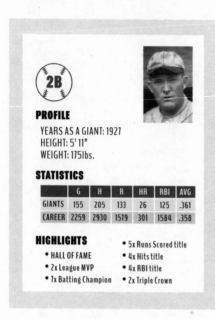

**PROFILE**
YEARS AS A GIANT: 1927
HEIGHT: 5' 11"
WEIGHT: 175lbs.

**STATISTICS**

|  | G | H | R | HR | RBI | AVG |
|---|---|---|---|---|---|---|
| GIANTS | 155 | 205 | 133 | 26 | 125 | .361 |
| CAREER | 2259 | 2930 | 1519 | 301 | 1584 | .358 |

**HIGHLIGHTS**
- HALL OF FAME
- 2x League MVP
- 7x Batting Champion
- 5x Runs Scored title
- 4x Hits title
- 4x RBI title
- 2x Triple Crown

Rogers Hornsby had an off-year offensively in 1926, his 12th season as a St. Louis Cardinal, as the .358 career hitter could "only" manage a .317 average with 11 home runs. During post-season negotiations for a new contract, Hornsby demanded $50,000 per year for three years. Cardinal ownership countered with a one-year contract for $50,000. When Hornsby refused to budge on his demands, the Cardinals traded the 30-year-old second baseman to the New York Giants for up-and-coming second baseman Frankie Frisch and Jimmy Ring on December 20, 1926.

Hornsby enjoyed a better season in 1927 as a Giant, as he hit .361 and led the league in runs scored (133), walks (86), and on-base percentage (.448). He also managed the Giants for part of the year while manager John McGraw dealt with health problems. However, Hornsby's gambling problems at the racetrack and distrust of Giants' management annoyed team owner Charles Stoneham. As a result, Hornsby was traded to the Boston Braves for Jimmy Welsh and Shanty Hogan during the offseason.

In addition to his .361 average and 133 runs scored, Hornsby knocked out 26 home runs and drove in 125 runs in his only season as a Giant. He went on to play 10 more seasons before retiring in 1937 after 23 years. His .358 lifetime batting average is still second all-time behind Ty Cobb's .367. Think about that: a .358 lifetime batting average over 23 seasons. Amazing.

Hogan actually had five respectable seasons while catching for the Giants, averaging .311 with 48 home runs and 333 RBIs in 618 games. Welsh, an outfielder, played in 162 games for the Giants over two seasons, hitting .294 with 11 home runs and 62 RBIs.

# JOHNNY MIZE

"The Big Cat" began his Hall-of-Fame career in 1936 with the St. Louis Cardinals, and one year later hit .364 to finish second in the National League batting title to teammate Joe Medwick who won with a .374 average. In 1939, Johnny Mize finished second in the league's MVP race voting after leading the league with a .349 average and 28 home runs. Mize's 43 home runs in 1940 set a Cardinals team record that stood for nearly 60 years. At the end of the 1941 season, which saw Mize hit .317 with 16 homers, Cardinals general manager Branch Rickey, who famously believed in trading players before their skills began to decline, traded the 29-year-old Mize to the Giants. In exchange for Mize, the Cardinals received Bill Lohrman, Johnny McCarthy, Ken O'Dea, and $50,000.

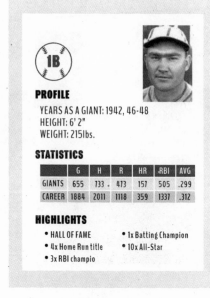

**PROFILE**
YEARS AS A GIANT: 1942, 46-48
HEIGHT: 6' 2"
WEIGHT: 215lbs.

**STATISTICS**

|        | G    | H    | R    | HR  | RBI  | AVG  |
|--------|------|------|------|-----|------|------|
| GIANTS | 655  | 733  | 473  | 157 | 505  | .299 |
| CAREER | 1884 | 2011 | 1118 | 359 | 1337 | .312 |

**HIGHLIGHTS**
- HALL OF FAME
- 4x Home Run title
- 3x RBI champio
- 1x Batting Champion
- 10x All-Star

In his first year as a Giant, Mize knocked out 26 home runs and 110 RBIs while hitting .305. The Big Cat then spent 1943 through 1945 in military service during World War II. Returning to the Giants in 1946, Mize hit .337 while falling one homer short of the home run title, won by Ralph Kiner of the Pittsburgh Pirates. In 1947 he bashed out 51 home runs and tied Kiner for the league lead. He also led the National League in runs and RBIs, and became the only player to strike out fewer than fifty times while hitting fifty home runs. Mize's 1947 totals in runs, home runs and RBI were all career highs.

By the time 1949 rolled around, the 36-year-old slugger's playing time began to be reduced as his batting average fell to .263. As a result, Mize was traded to the New York Yankees late in the 1949 season after expressing discontent with the decision to play him less. Although his playing time didn't increase much in the Bronx—he only played an average of 75 games a—it did give him the opportunity to play in the World Series for the first time in his career. And five in a row to boot. Mize retired after the 1953 season at the age of 40 after winning his fifth consecutive World Series championship with the Yankees.

# JOE MEDWICK

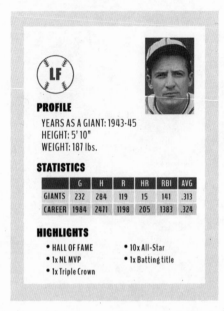

**PROFILE**
YEARS AS A GIANT: 1943-45
HEIGHT: 5' 10"
WEIGHT: 187 lbs.

**STATISTICS**

|  | G | H | R | HR | RBI | AVG |
|---|---|---|---|---|---|---|
| GIANTS | 232 | 284 | 119 | 15 | 141 | .313 |
| CAREER | 1984 | 2471 | 1198 | 205 | 1383 | .324 |

**HIGHLIGHTS**
- HALL OF FAME
- 1x NL MVP
- 1x Triple Crown
- 10x All-Star
- 1x Batting title

Like Rogers Hornsby and Johnny Mize before him, Joe Medwick's best days were with the St. Louis Cardinals before joining the Giants in mid-career. A rookie in 1932, Medwick's career began to take off in 1934 when he hit .319 with 106 RBIS, and peaked in 1937 when he won the National League Triple Crown for the Cardinals with a .374 average, 31 homers and 154 RBIs.

After a short stint with the Brooklyn Dodgers from 1940-1943, the 31-year-old Medwick was waived 48 games into the 1943 season after failing to hit any home runs and batting just .272. The Giants claimed him on July 16, 1943, and Medwick went on to play in 78 games the rest of that season, batting .281 with 5 home runs and 45 RBIs. In his only full season with the Giants the following year, Medwich batted .337 with 9 home runs and 85 RBIs. After playing 23 games in 1945, the Giants traded Medwick along with pitcher Ewald Pyle to the Boston Braves for catcher Clyde Kluttz. Kluttz played in 72 games over two seasons with the Giants, hitting .283 with four homers and 22 RBIs.

Medwick retired in 1948 at the age of 36 after playing 20 games with his original team, the St. Louis Cardinals.

# EDDIE STANKY

By the time Eddie Stanky was a member of the Giants in 1950, he had been a two-time All-Star with the Brooklyn Dodgers after breaking into the league with the Chicago Cubs in 1943. A .268 lifetime hitter, Stanky was best known for his ability to draw walks. In each of six different seasons, he drew 100 or more walks, 140 or more in two of them. In 1946 with the Dodgers, Stanky hit a mediocre .273 but his 137 walks gave him an on base percentage of .436 which edged out Stan Musial, who led the league in over ten hitting categories that season.

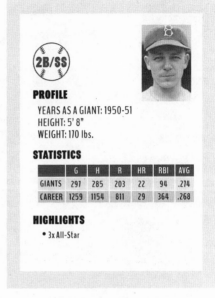

**2B/SS**

**PROFILE**
YEARS AS A GIANT: 1950-51
HEIGHT: 5' 8"
WEIGHT: 170 lbs.

**STATISTICS**

|  | G | H | R | HR | RBI | AVG |
|---|---|---|---|---|---|---|
| GIANTS | 297 | 285 | 203 | 22 | 94 | .274 |
| CAREER | 1259 | 1154 | 811 | 29 | 364 | .268 |

**HIGHLIGHTS**
• 3x All-Star

On December 14, 1949, the Boston Braves traded Stanky and Al Dark to the New York Giants for Sid Gordon, Buddy Kerr, Willard Marshall and Red Webb. A case could be made that his 1950 season with the Giants was the best in his career, when he hit an even .300 and led the league in walks (144) and OBP (.460). On August 30, he tied a major league record when he walked in seven consecutive at-bats.

Leo Durocher, who managed Stanky with the Dodgers and Giants, once said of him *"He can't hit, can't run, and can't field. He's no nice guy ... all the little SOB can do is win."* Stanky played in three World Series, including 1951 with the Giants. His teams lost all three.

Stank played two seasons with the Giants, hitting .274 in 297 games with 22 home runs and 94 RBIs, before being traded to the St. Louis Cardinals in 1952. He retired after the 1953 season at the age of 37.

# HARVEY KUENN

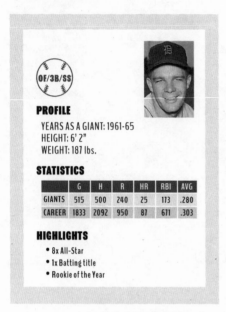

**PROFILE**
YEARS AS A GIANT: 1961-65
HEIGHT: 6' 2"
WEIGHT: 187 lbs.

**STATISTICS**

|  | G | H | R | HR | RBI | AVG |
|---|---|---|---|---|---|---|
| GIANTS | 515 | 500 | 240 | 25 | 173 | .280 |
| CAREER | 1833 | 2092 | 950 | 87 | 611 | .303 |

**HIGHLIGHTS**
- 8x All-Star
- 1x Batting title
- Rookie of the Year

Harvey Kuenn's baseball career got off to a roaring start in 1952 when, as a rookie with the Detroit Tigers, he knocked out a league high 209 hits while batting .308. He followed that up with 201 hits and a .306 average in his sophomore year. Kuenn was an All-Star those two seasons and the next six, including one with Cleveland, who he was surprisingly traded to in 1959 for fan favorite Rocky Colavito just two days before the start of the season. Colavito had just won the American League home run title with 42, while Kuenn captured the American League batting crown in with a .353 average.

Kuenn hit .308 in his only season as an Indian before Cleveland sent him to the Giants on December 3, 1960 for Johnny Antonelli and Willie Kirkland. Kuenn went on to hit .280 in five seasons with the Giants, including .304 in 1962 when he belted 10 home runs and drove in 68 runs, the most as a Giant. Kuenn had the dubious distinction of making the final out in two of Sandy Koufax's four no-hitters—in 1963 and 1965.

The Giants traded Kuenn to the Chicago Cubs in 1965, where he played the parts of two seasons with the Cubs and one with the Philadelphia Phillies before retiring after the 1966 season at the age of 35.

# ED BAILEY

After spending his first nine seasons as a Cincinnati Red, the 30-year-old, four-time All-Star was traded to the catcher-hungry Giants on April 27, 1961 for Don Blasingame, Bob Schmidt and Sherman Jones. Ed Bailey appeared in his only World Series in 1962 with the Giants, playing in six games and knocking out a homer in game 3 against the Yankees.

Bailey never played in more than 107 games in any one of his four seasons in San Francisco, as he primarily platooned with fellow lefty hitting catcher Tom Haller, but was named an All-Star in 1963 when he batted .263 with 21 home runs and 68 RBIs.

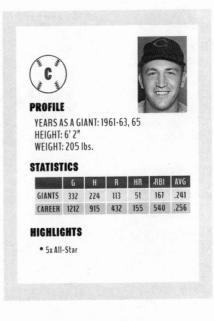

**PROFILE**
YEARS AS A GIANT: 1961-63, 65
HEIGHT: 6' 2"
WEIGHT: 205 lbs.

**STATISTICS**

|  | G | H | R | HR | RBI | AVG |
|---|---|---|---|---|---|---|
| GIANTS | 332 | 224 | 113 | 51 | 167 | .241 |
| CAREER | 1212 | 915 | 432 | 155 | 540 | .256 |

**HIGHLIGHTS**
• 5x All-Star

In December 1962, the Giants traded Bailey, Felipe Alou and Billy Hoeft to the Atlanta Braves for Del Crandell, Bob Hendley and Bob Shaw. Two years later on February 1, 1965, the Braves sent him back to the Giants for former ace Billy O'Dell. Fourteen games into the 1965 season, the Giants sent Bailey, Hendley, and Harvey Kuenn to the Chicago Cubs for Dick Bertell and Len Gabrielson. Bailey ended his world-wind career on May 7, 1966 after playing five games with the California Angels.

In total, Bailey played in 332 games as a San Francisco Giant, batting .261 with 51 home runs and 167 RBIs.

# SAM MCDOWELL

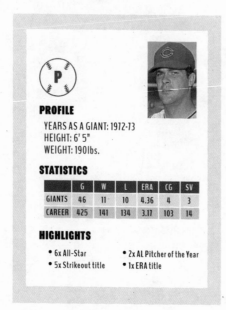

**PROFILE**
YEARS AS A GIANT: 1972-73
HEIGHT: 6' 5"
WEIGHT: 190lbs.

**STATISTICS**

|  | G | W | L | ERA | CG | SV |
|---|---|---|---|---|---|---|
| GIANTS | 46 | 11 | 10 | 4.36 | 4 | 3 |
| CAREER | 425 | 141 | 134 | 3.17 | 103 | 14 |

**HIGHLIGHTS**

- 6x All-Star
- 5x Strikeout title
- 2x AL Pitcher of the Year
- 1x ERA title

"Sudden Sam" McDowell, an imposing 6'5" lefty nicknamed such because of his slow wind up and electrifying fastball, was a dominating presence in the American League during the mid-1960's and early 1970's for a lowly Cleveland Indians ball club. From 1965-1971, McDowell was an all-star six times, won an ERA title (2.18 in 1965), and was a 20-game winner in 1970 for a team that won 76 games. He also led the league in strikeouts-per-nine-innings ratio six times during that period.

By the time 1972 rolled along, however, the 29-year-old McDowell's fastball began to lose steam, and his dominance was starting to fade. In 1971, his record slipped to 13-17 while walking a career high 153 batters. After some contract issues with the Indians and the American League, McDowell demanded a trade after the 1971 season. The Giants, seeing an opportunity to deal an aging 33-year-old, 10-year veteran hurler for a younger flame thrower, dealt Gaylord Perry (16-12, 2.76 ERA in 1971) and infielder Frank Duffy to Cleveland for McDowell.

The trade, in hindsight, would go down as one of the worst trades in Giants history, as Perry went on to win 180 more games in his career while McDowell would win only 24 more. McDowell lasted only a season-and-a-half in San Francisco, winning 11 games, losing 10 and forking out a 4.36 ERA, before being sold to the New York Yankees on June 7, 1973. Injuries began to plague him, and after playing 43 games with the Yankees and Pittsburgh Pirates, McDowell was forced to retire in 1975 at the age of 32.

Perry, on the other hand went 24–16 in 1972 with a 1.92 ERA and one save in his first year with Cleveland, winning his first Cy Young Award. Ouch.

# BOBBY MERCER

In 1969 when rookie Bobby Mercer took centerfield for the New York Yankees, he had big shoes to fill. Mickey Mantle, the Hall-of-Fame legend had retired the year before, and Bobby Mercer was being touted as the next Mickey Mantle. Unfair as that was, Mercer responded by hitting 22 or more home runs his first five seasons as a Yankee. He drove in over 90 runs three times, and hit over .300 twice, including .331 in 1971. He was also an All-Star four of his first six seasons.

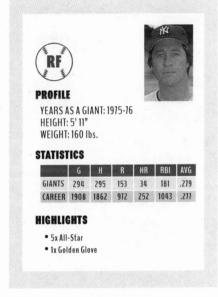

**PROFILE**
YEARS AS A GIANT: 1975-76
HEIGHT: 5' 11"
WEIGHT: 160 lbs.

**STATISTICS**

|  | G | H | R | HR | RBI | AVG |
|---|---|---|---|---|---|---|
| GIANTS | 294 | 295 | 153 | 34 | 181 | .279 |
| CAREER | 1908 | 1862 | 912 | 252 | 1043 | .277 |

**HIGHLIGHTS**
- 5x All-Star
- 1x Golden Glove

Bobby Bonds, like Mercer, was following in the footsteps of a legend as well: one Willie Mays. After playing in 81 games in 1968, Bonds took over right field in 1969 for good. In his seven years as a Giant, Bonds hit over 20 home runs in six of them, including 30 or more in 1969, 1971 and 1973. He was an All-Star twice, an All-Star MVP once, and a three-time Golden Glove winner. Bonds also had the distinction of leading the league in strikeouts three times, striking out over 130 times in each of his seasons in San Francisco.

After the 1974 season, however, the Yankees were looking for more right-handed power, and the Giants more consistency. So, the two clubs surprised the baseball world by swapping their star outfielders in a straight up trade of $100,000 superstars.

Mercer spent two years in San Francisco, becoming an All-Star in his first season when he hit .298 with 11 home runs and 91 RBIs. After knocking out 23 home runs and driving in 90 runs in his second season, Mercer was traded to the Chicago Cubs with Steve Ontiveros for reining National League batting champ Bill Matlock and Rob Sperring on February 11, 1977. Mercer returned to the Yankees in 1979 and played four more seasons with New York before retiring in 1983. Madlock played three seasons in San Francisco, hitting .296 in 331 games.

Bonds only played one year in New York, hitting .270 with 32 home runs and 85 RBIs while making the All-Star team as well, before being shipped to the California Angels for Mickey Rivers and Ed Figueroa on December 11, 1975. Bonds went on to play for five more teams before retiring in 1981.

# JOE MORGAN

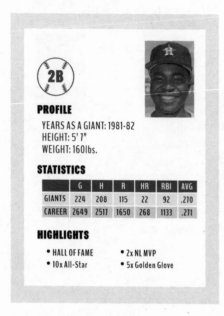

**2B**

**PROFILE**
YEARS AS A GIANT: 1981-82
HEIGHT: 5' 7"
WEIGHT: 160 lbs.

**STATISTICS**

|  | G | H | R | HR | RBI | AVG |
|---|---|---|---|---|---|---|
| GIANTS | 224 | 208 | 115 | 22 | 92 | .270 |
| CAREER | 2649 | 2517 | 1650 | 268 | 1133 | .271 |

**HIGHLIGHTS**

- HALL OF FAME
- 10x All-Star
- 2x NL MVP
- 5x Golden Glove

By the time Joe Morgan joined the Giants as a free agent on February 9, 1981, he was 37-years old and about to start his 19th year in the big leagues. The 5'7, 160 pound powerhouse's best days were well behind him. But he could still contribute, and his leadership skills were priceless. And that's just what the young 1981 Giants team needed. After a slow start during the first half of the 1981 strike-plagued season where Major League Baseball actually played two individual halves, the Giants finished the second half six games over .500 and third place in the National League West. They followed that up with an 89-73 1982, the first time they finished over .500 for a complete season since 1978.

Although Morgan's tenure with the Giants was short, he'll always be a hero to Giants fans when on the last game of 1982 his 7th inning home run broke a 2-2 tie that ultimately gave the Giants a 5-3 victory over the Los Angeles Dodgers and eliminate them from the division race. That would be Morgan's last at-bat as a San Francisco Giant, as he was united with former Reds teammates Pete Rose and Tony Perez in Philadelphia on December 14, 1982 when the Giants traded him and pitcher Al Holland to the Phillies for Mike Krukow, Mark Davis and C.L. Penigar. Morgan had sought a $600,000 contract for the coming season while the Giants offered $450,000. As a result, Morgan's agent announced that he would go to salary arbitration, and the Giants decided to trade him instead.

In 224 games with the Giants, Morgan hit .270 with 22 home runs and 92 RBIs. He was elected to the Major League Baseball Hall-of-Fame in 1990.

# AL OLIVER

In 1983, 36-year-old Al Oliver hit an even .300, drove in 84 runs, and made the All-Star team for the Montreal Expos. In 1984, however, the Expos decided to move in the direction of youth, and started to deal away some of their veteran players. So, on February 27, 1984, the Expos peddled Oliver to the Giants for pitchers Fred Breining, Andy McGaffigan and young outfielder Max Venable.

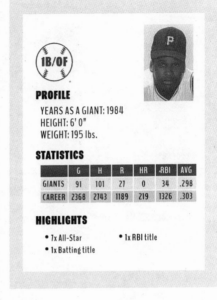

**1B/OF**

**PROFILE**
YEARS AS A GIANT: 1984
HEIGHT: 6' 0"
WEIGHT: 195 lbs.

**STATISTICS**

|  | G | H | R | HR | RBI | AVG |
|---|---|---|---|---|---|---|
| GIANTS | 91 | 101 | 27 | 0 | 34 | .298 |
| CAREER | 2368 | 2743 | 1189 | 219 | 1326 | .303 |

**HIGHLIGHTS**
- 1x All-Star
- 1x RBI title
- 1x Batting title

Oliver's tenure on the Giants lasted a mere 91 games, as on August 21, he was involved in one of the shortest trades in baseball history, some 500 feet, to the visiting Philadelphia Phillies. He responded by ripping a two-run double to lead his new club to a 6-4 triumph over the Giants. Although batting .298 at the time, the Giants were hungry for pitchers and dealt Oliver for minor-league pitchers George Riley and Kelly Downs. Downs went on to be a three time 10+ game winner for the Giants, including a 13-9, 3.32 ERA campaign in 1988. Oliver would retire after the 1985 season with the Toronto Blue Jays following a short stint with the Los Angeles Dodgers.

In his 91 games as a Giant, Oliver had 101 hits for a .298 average. He also drove in 34 runs while hitting no round trippers.

# MANNY TRILLO

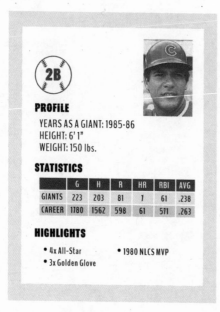

**2B**

**PROFILE**
YEARS AS A GIANT: 1985-86
HEIGHT: 6'1"
WEIGHT: 150 lbs.

**STATISTICS**

|  | G | H | R | HR | RBI | AVG |
|---|---|---|---|---|---|---|
| GIANTS | 223 | 203 | 81 | 7 | 61 | .238 |
| CAREER | 1780 | 1562 | 598 | 61 | 571 | .263 |

**HIGHLIGHTS**

- 4x All-Star
- 3x Golden Glove
- 1980 NLCS MVP

After three straight All-Star seasons and capturing the 1980 NLCS MVP award to help lead the Philadelphia Phillies to their first World Series championship since their conception in 1883, Trillo was traded with four other players to the Cleveland Indians for highly touted rookie Von Hayes following the 1982 season. Ironically, the Giants helped the Phillies find their second base replacement, as they traded Joe Morgan to the Philadelphia following failed contract negotiations with the future Hall-of-Famer.

After splitting time with the Indians and Montreal Expos in 1983, the Giants picked up the 33-year-old 11-year veteran as a free agent on December 20, 1983 to partially help fill the hole left by Joe Morgan the year before.

Trillo's career actually began with the Oakland Athletics in 1973 and he participated, albeit briefly, in both their 1973 and 1974 post seasons. Playing primarily in the minors during 1973, Trillo was left off of the World Series roster against the New York Mets. However, in game 2 when A's second baseman Mike Andrews committed two errors in a 12-inning loss, an angry A's owner Charles Finley notoriously attempted to waive Andrews onto the disabled list in order to activate Trillo, which then commissioner Bowie Kuhn disallowed.

In the 1974 post season, Trillo played in one game against Baltimore in the ALCS, but did not appear in the World Series against the Los Angeles Dodgers.

For the Giants, Trillo played in 223 games over two seasons, knocking out 203 hits while hitting .238 with seven home runs and 61 RBI. On December 11, 1985, the San Francisco traded the 34-year-old Trillo to the Cubs for 27-year-old infielder Dave Owen. Owen, who had played in 85 games in three years for the Cubs, was subsequently released by the Giants on March 24, 1986. After playing in seven games for the Kansas City Royals in 1988, Owen disappeared from Major League baseball.

Trillo played three seasons with the Cubs before retiring as a Cincinnati Red in 1989 at age 38.

# STEVE CARLTON

Between 1971 and 1982, there was no pitcher more dominant than Steve "Lefty" Carlton: a 20-game winner six times, a Cy Young winner four times, and an All-Star 10 times. In 1972, Carlton had one of the amazing years in baseball history for a hurler when he pitched a whopping 346 innings, won 27 games, and posted a 1.97 ERA. And all for a Philadelphia Phillies team that won 57 games all year. That's right, Carlton single handedly won nearly half of the team's games that season.

Fast forward to 1986, and Carlton, still a Philly, had posted a 4-8 record and 5.89 ERA through the first half of the

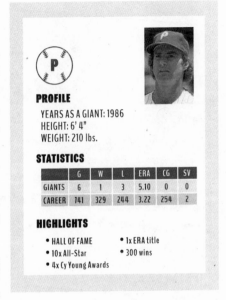

**PROFILE**
YEARS AS A GIANT: 1986
HEIGHT: 6' 4"
WEIGHT: 210 lbs.

**STATISTICS**

|  | G | W | L | ERA | CG | SV |
|---|---|---|---|---|---|---|
| GIANTS | 6 | 1 | 3 | 5.10 | 0 | 0 |
| CAREER | 741 | 329 | 244 | 3.22 | 254 | 2 |

**HIGHLIGHTS**
- HALL OF FAME
- 10x All-Star
- 4x Cy Young Awards
- 1x ERA title
- 300 wins

season. Now 41 years old, Carlton watched his ERA steadily climb since the 1982 season. As a result, the Phillies decided to part ways with their long time ace and released him on June 24, 1986. Ten days later, the Giants picked up the future Hall of Famer, hoping that a change of scenery might stimulate Carlton's career. But after six starts, it became apparent that wouldn't be the case, as Carlton went 1-3 with a 5.10 ERA, giving up 36 hits and 20 runs in 30 innings. So, after a month of unproductively, the Giants decided to part ways and released Carlton on August 12, 1986.

However, his month with the Giants wasn't without a couple of highlights. First, and foremost, Carlton struck out his 4,000th hitter; becoming only the second pitcher in baseball history to do so (Nolan Ryan beat him by a year). He's still only one of four pitchers to have achieved that. And in his only win as a Giant, Carlton pitched seven innings of shutout ball in a start against the Pittsburgh Pirates while hitting a 3-run homer.

Carlton finished the season with the Chicago White Sox and started 32 more games in the next two years for both the Cleveland Indians and Minnesota Twins before retiring in 1988.

# RICH GOSSAGE

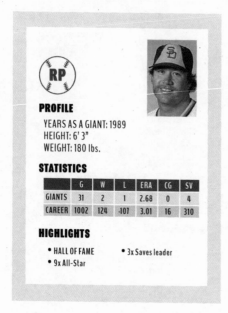

## PROFILE
YEARS AS A GIANT: 1989
HEIGHT: 6' 3"
WEIGHT: 180 lbs.

## STATISTICS

|  | G | W | L | ERA | CG | SV |
|---|---|---|---|---|---|---|
| GIANTS | 31 | 2 | 1 | 2.68 | 0 | 4 |
| CAREER | 1002 | 124 | -107 | 3.01 | 16 | 310 |

## HIGHLIGHTS

• HALL OF FAME   • 3x Saves leader
• 9x All-Star

Along with Rollie Fingers, Rich "Goose" Gossage is regarded as one of the pioneers of the closer role during his time with the New York Yankees in the 1970's. Nicknamed "Goose" when a friend of his didn't like the nickname "Goss," and then changed it because he thought Gossage looked like a goose when he extended his neck to read the signs given by the catcher when he was pitching.

During his career that included time with nine teams, Gossage pitched in 1,002 games and finished 681 of them, earning 310 saves. Gossage logged 53 seven-plus out saves in his career, something unheard of today. In comparison, Mariano Rivera, the current all-time Saves leader, only did that once in his 19-year career. On August 6, 1988, while with the Cubs, Gossage became the second pitcher to record 300 career saves, following Rollie Fingers achievement six years earlier. On August 17, 1986, Gossage struck out Pete Rose in Rose's final major-league at bat.

After the Cubs released Gossage following spring training in 1989, the Giants signed the righty reliever on April 14. During the 31 games he pitched with the team that season, Gossage racked up four saves in 31 games. He struck out 24 in 43 innings, going 2-1 with a 2.68 ERA. On June 18, the Giants picked up All-Star closer Steve Bedrosian from the Philadelphia Phillies in a trade, making Gossage expendable. After being released by the Giants on August 10, 1989, the Goose went on to play four more seasons, two with Oakland and one with Texas and Seattle, before retiring in 1994 at the age of 42.

Gossage was a nine time All-Star, three-time Save leader, and pitched in three World Series during his 14 year Hall-of-Fame career.

# GARY CARTER

In 1977, 23-year-old Gary "Kid" Carter's Hall-of-Fame career took off. Hitting .284 with 31 home runs and 84 RBIs, Carter began giving fellow National League catcher Johnny Bench something he'd yet experience as a pro: serious competition for starting catcher in the All-Star game. Carter went on to play in 10 straight All-Star games from 1979-1988, supplanting Bench for good when the long time Red retired in 1983.

After a stellar career in Montreal, the Expos traded Carter to the Mets following the 1984 season after turning down Carter's salary demands. "Kid" went on to have three strong seasons with the

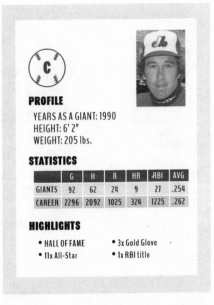

**PROFILE**
YEARS AS A GIANT: 1990
HEIGHT: 6' 2"
WEIGHT: 205 lbs.

**STATISTICS**

| | G | H | R | HR | RBI | AVG |
|---|---|---|---|---|---|---|
| GIANTS | 92 | 62 | 24 | 9 | 27 | .254 |
| CAREER | 2296 | 2092 | 1025 | 324 | 1225 | .262 |

**HIGHLIGHTS**
- HALL OF FAME
- 11x All-Star
- 3x Gold Glove
- 1x RBI title

Mets, and picked up his first and only World Series ring in 1986. By 1988, injuries began to plague the 34-year-old backstop, and after only playing in 50 games in 1989, the Mets cut ties with their aging catcher.

The Giants signed Carter on January 19, 1990, and then platooned him with left-handed hitting Terry Kennedy throughout the 1990 season. Carter played in 92 games with San Francisco that year, clubbing out nine home runs, driving in 27, and hitting .254. After the Giants released him on November 5, 1990, the Dodgers signed him for the 1991 season. Carter then rejoined the Expos for 95 games in 1992 before retiring after the season ended. Ironically, Carter's final hit came on September 27, 1992 when he hit a double over the head of former Expo teammate Andre Dawson of the Chicago Cubs.

# DARRYL STRAWBERRY

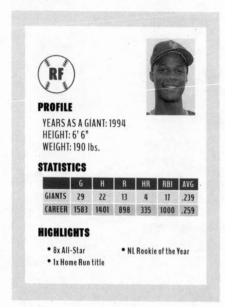

**PROFILE**
YEARS AS A GIANT: 1994
HEIGHT: 6' 6"
WEIGHT: 190 lbs.

**STATISTICS**

|  | G | H | R | HR | RBI | AVG |
|---|---|---|---|---|---|---|
| GIANTS | 29 | 22 | 13 | 4 | 17 | .239 |
| CAREER | 1583 | 1401 | 898 | 335 | 1000 | .259 |

**HIGHLIGHTS**

- 8x All-Star
- 1x Home Run title
- NL Rookie of the Year

Darryl Strawberry was undoubtedly one of the best, exciting, and most popular baseball players in the 1980's. After winning National League Rookie-of-the-Year in 1983, Strawberry went on to blast 26 or more home runs in each of the next eight seasons, including a league high 39 in 1988.

A lucrative offer by the Los Angeles Dodgers drew the free agent to the west coast after the 1990 season, where he knocked out 28 home runs in his first year as a Dodger. By the end of the 1991 season, he had accumulated 280 home runs by the age of 29 and was starting to draw comparison to home run king Hank Aaron. However, injuries and personal problems would begin to affect Strawberry's production, and he wound up only playing in 75 games the next two seasons. On May 24, 1994, he was released by the Dodgers and signed by the Giants on June 19, who were looking to add some pop along side Barry Bonds. After finishing the season with San Francisco, he was released on February 8, 1995.

In 29 games with the Giants, Strawberry hit four home runs, drove in 17 while hitting .239. He went on to sign with the New York Yankees in 1995 and played with them until he retired in 1999.

# DEION SANDERS

The city of San Francisco had a dream in 1995: to make Deion Sanders a full-time player in their city. Sanders, a two-way athlete, was already a Pro Bowl corner-back in the NFL, and had just helped the 49ers win the 1994-95 Super Bowl. Sanders also had been playing Major League Baseball since 1989 when he was signed by the New York Yankees. Currently, however, he was a member of the Cincinnati Reds, and the Giants wanted him in San Francisco. Plus the Giants needed him, as fan interest in the team was at an all-time low as less than 15,000 fans on average were attending home games.

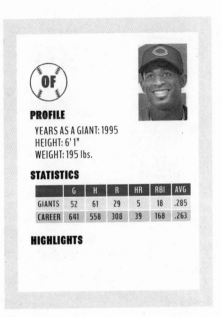

**PROFILE**
YEARS AS A GIANT: 1995
HEIGHT: 6' 1"
WEIGHT: 195 lbs.

**STATISTICS**

|  | G | H | R | HR | RBI | AVG |
|---|---|---|---|---|---|---|
| GIANTS | 52 | 61 | 29 | 5 | 18 | .285 |
| CAREER | 641 | 558 | 308 | 39 | 168 | .263 |

**HIGHLIGHTS**

On July 21, 1995, the Giants sent three pretty good players, Dave Burba, Mark Portugal, and outfielder Darren Lewis to the Reds for Sanders and four minor league players. Sanders went on to play 52 games for the Giants that year, hitting .285 with five home runs and 18 RBIs while occupying the leadoff spot.

However, the city's dream of signing the speedster to both a longer-term baseball and football deal was short-lived as Sanders, a free agent in the NFL, was swayed by a $35 million, 7-year offer from the Dallas Cowboys and signed with them in September, 1995. By then, Sanders also decided to focus more on football and didn't play baseball again until 1997 when he returned to Cincinnati for 115 games, and then for 32 more in 2001 with the Reds before retiring for good from baseball.

# OREL HERSHISER

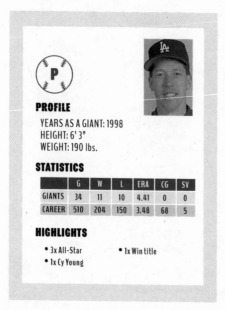

**PROFILE**
YEARS AS A GIANT: 1998
HEIGHT: 6' 3"
WEIGHT: 190 lbs.

**STATISTICS**

|        | G   | W   | L   | ERA  | CG | SV |
|--------|-----|-----|-----|------|----|----|
| GIANTS | 34  | 11  | 10  | 4.41 | 0  | 0  |
| CAREER | 510 | 204 | 150 | 3.48 | 68 | 5  |

**HIGHLIGHTS**

- 3x All-Star
- 1x Cy Young
- 1x Win title

Although Orel Hershiser played for 18 seasons, he's really best known for three: 1985, 1988 and 1995. In 1985, his third in the majors, the 26-year-old Hershiser had a phenomenal season, going 19-3 with a microscopic 2.03 ERA. After two .500 seasons, Hershiser would re-emerge in 1988 by winning the Cy Young award, going 23-8 with a 2.28 ERA.

Following shoulder re-construction surgery in 1990, Hershiser rejoined the Dodgers in 1991 and was a mediocre pitcher for the next four seasons, winning 35 games overall with ERAs of 3.46 or above. After the 1994 season, the Dodgers cut ties with their former superstar, and on April 8, 1995 Hershiser signed as a free agent with the Cleveland Indians. With his career resurrected, Hershiser posted a 16-6 record for the Indians, helping lead them to their first World Series appearance in 41 years (they would lose to the Atlanta Braves in six games). He won two games in the American League Championship series against Seattle and was named Most Valuable Player. By doing so, Hershiser became first player to win the League Championship MVP Award in both leagues.

After going 14-6 with the Indians in 1997, Hershiser became a free agent, and on December 9, 1997, the 39-year-old signed with the Giants. Hershiser played one season for San Francisco, going 11-10 with a 4.41 ERA in 34 starts. He struck out 126 batters in 202 innings, the last time he would reach 200 innings in his career. His contract actually contained an option for 1999 but the Giants declined it after the season, although they stated an interested in coming to terms on a new deal. Instead, Hershiser signed a minor league contract to rejoin the Indians on February 20, 1999.

After being cut by the Indians in spring training, Hershiser signed with Mets where he posted a 13-12 record in 1999 before becoming a free agent again. Prior to the 2000 season, Hershiser went full circle, once again returning to the Dodgers. After going 1-5 with a 13.14 ERA, the Dodgers released him on June 27, 2000, and on July 6, Hershiser announced his retirement from baseball.

# ANDRES GALARRAGA

After spending 15 productive years in the National League that featured five All-Star games, two gold gloves, two RBI titles, a home run title, a batting title, and a battle with lymphatic cancer that benched him for the entire 1999 season, Andres "Big Cat" Galarraga (so named because of his defensive quickness while playing first base) opted for free agency after the 2000 season when his current team, the Atlanta Braves, wouldn't give the him a two year deal. The 40-year-old soon found a suitor in the Texas Rangers of the American League.

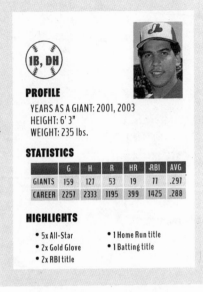

**1B, DH**

**PROFILE**
YEARS AS A GIANT: 2001, 2003
HEIGHT: 6' 3"
WEIGHT: 235 lbs.

**STATISTICS**

|  | G | H | R | HR | RBI | AVG |
|---|---|---|---|---|---|---|
| GIANTS | 159 | 127 | 53 | 19 | 77 | .297 |
| CAREER | 2257 | 2333 | 1195 | 399 | 1425 | .288 |

**HIGHLIGHTS**

- 5x All-Star
- 2x Gold Glove
- 2x RBI title
- 1 Home Run title
- 1 Batting title

Halfway through the 2001 season, however, Galarraga's role with the team diminished into backing up Rafael Palmeiro with an occasional start as their designated hitter. As he continued to struggle with American League pitching, the Rangers decided to deal the .235 hitting "Big Cat" to the Giants on July 24, 2001 for three minor leaguers. Galarraga finished the year with San Francisco hitting .288 with seven home runs and 35 RBIs before re-signing with his original team, the Montreal Expos, in March 2002. But his relationship with the Giants wasn't over.

In early 2003 after Montreal decided not to resign him, San Francisco invited Galarraga to spring training where he would sign a minor league contract for the 2003 season. Galarraga ended up playing in 110 games for the Giants in his second stint with the team, batting .301 with 12 home runs and 42 RBIs. He would play three games with the Anaheim Angels in 2004 before retiring from baseball.

# OMAR VIZQUEL

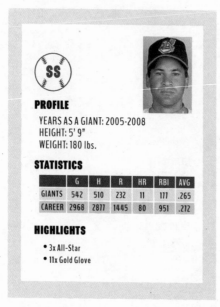

**PROFILE**
YEARS AS A GIANT: 2005-2008
HEIGHT: 5' 9"
WEIGHT: 180 lbs.

**STATISTICS**

|  | G | H | R | HR | RBI | AVG |
|---|---|---|---|---|---|---|
| GIANTS | 542 | 510 | 232 | 11 | 177 | .265 |
| CAREER | 2968 | 2877 | 1445 | 80 | 951 | .272 |

**HIGHLIGHTS**

• 3x All-Star
• 11x Gold Glove

Noted particularly for his defense, Omar Vizquel won nine Golden Glove awards for his fielding during the 16 years he played for the Seattle Mariners and Cleveland Indians in the American League. He also played in three All-Star games during that part of his career, which began as a rookie with the Mariners in 1989.

Vizquel was traded to the Indians after the 1993 season where he began a storied 11-year career with the Ohio team. But in 2003, injuries began to take its toll on the 36-year-old shortstop. Despite playing in 148 games in 2004, the Indians decided to part ways with their aging free agent to be.

On November 7, 2004, the Giants stepped in and signed the 38-year-old veteran, hoping to revive his career and bring in some additional leadership to the team; just as they did in recent years with players like Joe Morgan.

During his four seasons with the Giants, the slick fielding shortstop played in over 145 games in three of the seasons, knocking in over 54 runs in two of them, while hitting .295 in 2006. He also snagged two more Golden Glove awards in 2005 and 2006, making him one of the few shortstops to win a Golden Glove in both leagues. He also became the oldest to win as well, as he was 39-years old when he won the second one. Injuries again began to nag the aging shortstop, now 41-years-old, limiting him to just 92 games in 2008. As a result, the Giants elected to not resign the fan favorite after that season.

Vizquel went on to play with the Texas Rangers and Chicago White Sox before retiring as a Toronto Blue Jay after the 2012 season at the age of 45. On June 25, 2010, Vizquel hit his first homer of the season to make him only one of four players in MLB history to hit a home run in four different decades (with Ted Williams, Willie McCovey and Rickey Henderson). Who would have guessed that!

Vizquel finished his career in 2012 with Toronto, where the 45-year-old played 60 games for the Blue Jays.

# MIGUEL TEJADA

By the end of the 2003 season, Miguel Tejada had established himself as one of baseball's premier shortstops while a member of the Oakland Athletics. But when the A's elected not to re-sign the free agent, citing budget concerns and a young-and-coming minor league prospect named Bobby Crosby, Tejada signed a six-year, $72 million deal with the Baltimore Orioles during the 2004 offseason. In his last five seasons with the A's, Tejada had won league MVP in 2002, while averaging 29 home runs and 110 RBIS a season during that span. He also led the league in games played six straight seasons (2001-06) with Oakland

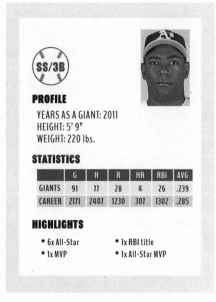

**SS/3B**

**PROFILE**
YEARS AS A GIANT: 2011
HEIGHT: 5' 9"
WEIGHT: 220 lbs.

**STATISTICS**

|  | G | H | R | HR | RBI | AVG |
|---|---|---|---|---|---|---|
| GIANTS | 91 | 77 | 28 | 4 | 26 | .239 |
| CAREER | 2171 | 2407 | 1230 | 307 | 1302 | .285 |

**HIGHLIGHTS**
- 6x All-Star
- 1x MVP
- 1x RBI title
- 1x All-Star MVP

and Baltimore. Tejada made the A's regret their decision immediately, as he had his best career year in his first season with Baltimore, blasting 34 homers, 150 RBIs and hitting .311.

By the time the Giants signed him as a free agent in 2011, Tejada was 37-years old and his production had been on the decline. In the previous season with the San Diego Padres, his average had dropped to .269 while hitting 15 homers, which was the third season in a row he had hit 15 or fewer long bombs.

Granted free agency from the Padres after the 2010 season, Tejada signed a one year $6.5 million contract with the Giants on Dec. 2, 2010, as the Giants front office were hoping to repeat the magic of their signing of 38-year-old shortstop Omar Vizquel six years earlier, who wound up contributing four good seasons for the Giants. Tejada, however, was unable to finish the 2011 season, partly due to a lower abdominal strain which caused him to miss 25 games, and was released on September 8, 2011. During the 91 games he played for the Giants, Tejada hit .239 with four homers and 26 RBIs. He retired in 2013 after playing in 53 games with the Kansas City Royals.

# CARLOS BELTRAN

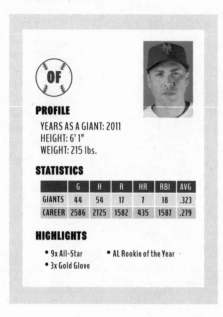

**OF**

**PROFILE**
YEARS AS A GIANT: 2011
HEIGHT: 6' 1"
WEIGHT: 215 lbs.

**STATISTICS**

|  | G | H | R | HR | RBI | AVG |
|---|---|---|---|---|---|---|
| GIANTS | 44 | 54 | 17 | 7 | 18 | .323 |
| CAREER | 2586 | 2725 | 1582 | 435 | 1587 | .279 |

**HIGHLIGHTS**

- 9x All-Star
- 3x Gold Glove
- AL Rookie of the Year

After catcher Buster Posey went down with a season-ending leg injury following a ferocious home plate collision on May 26, 2011, the defending World Series Champion Giants went out looking for hitting help. And on July 28, 2011, they landed one of the biggest fish in the ocean at that time. After waiving his no-trade clause, the Mets traded All-Star outfielder Carlos Beltrán to the Giants in exchange for their top pitching prospect, Zack Wheeler. The move was deemed a bit of a gamble for San Francisco, as Beltran was a 37-year-old free agent after the season, and the Giants were risking getting a "rental" player for three months at the expense of a top-rated young pitcher.

For the rest of the 2011 season with the Giants, Beltrán played in 44 games and batted .323 with seven home runs and 18 RBI. Beltrán wasn't enough to push the Giants to a National League West title, however, as they finished 86-76, eight games back of the first place Arizona Diamondbacks.

During the offseason, Beltrán maintained in the press that he had enjoyed his time in San Francisco and wanted to play for a contender, which the Giants certainly were as they had won the World Series the year before and were primed to do so again. But the Giants opted instead to invest their money on keeping their pitching staff intact.

Beltrán went on to sign a two-year, $26 million deal with the St. Louis Cardinals, in which he would be an All-Star both years. Ironically, the Giants and Cardinals would face off against each other in 2012 for the National League Pennant, which the Giants would win 4 games to 3 after battling back from a 3-1 deficit. Beltran played in six of the games, batting .300, knocking out one homer and driving in two runs in the series. He retired with the Houston Astros after 2017 season.

What happened to Zack Wheeler? As of 2019 he's still playing for the New York Mets, although his career has been injury-filled so far. After missing the entire 2015 and 2016 seasons, After pitching in 17 games in 2017, the now 29-year-old had his best season in 2018 when he went 12-7 with a 3.3.1 ERA.

# THE END OF THE LINE

In the 1950's and 1960's, the Giants were more often than not engaged in a battle for the National League pennant. During that time, as you'll soon discover, the Giants would frequently bring on a player in the twilight of their career who was hungry for one final championship run. The hope was that their experience, and motivation to win one final time, would give the team an added edge during a pennant drive.

The following are 15 notable players who, although ending their careers with the Giants, enjoyed their most productive, glory-filled, or at least memorable years with other teams.

- Carl Mays
- Tony Lazzeri
- Gabby Hartnett
- Ernie Lombardi
- Vince DiMaggio
- Joe Garagiola
- Jackie Robinson
- Hank Sauer
- Duke Snider
- Warren Spahn
- Dick Groat
- Dan Quisenberry
- Joe Carter
- Eric Davis
- Randy Johnson

# CARL MAYS

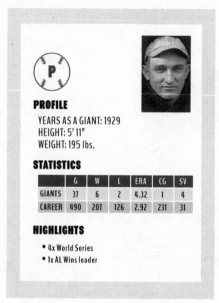

**PROFILE**
YEARS AS A GIANT: 1929
HEIGHT: 5' 11"
WEIGHT: 195 lbs.

**STATISTICS**

|  | G | W | L | ERA | CG | SV |
|---|---|---|---|---|---|---|
| GIANTS | 37 | 6 | 2 | 4.32 | 1 | 4 |
| CAREER | 490 | 207 | 126 | 2.92 | 231 | 31 |

**HIGHLIGHTS**

- 4x World Series
- 1x AL Wins leader

In a 15-year career with the Boston Red Sox, New York Yankees, Cincinnati Reds, and New York Giants, Carl Mays compiled a 207–126 record with 29 shutouts, 862 strikeouts and a 2.92 earned run average at a time when the league ERA average was 3.48. He won twenty or more games five times, including a league high 27 in 1921.

Mays was also pretty good with a bat, hitting five home runs, driving in 110 runs while supporting a lifetime .268 batting average, unheard of for a pitcher these days. And speaking of unheard of in today's baseball world, as a Red Sox, Mays once tossed two nine-inning complete game victories on the same day, beating the Philadelphia Athletics 12–0 and 4–1 on August 30, 1918.

Although he did win over 200 games, Mays is primarily remembered for throwing the pitch that killed Ray Chapman of the Cleveland Indians on August 16, 1920. Chapman became the only Major League player to die as a direct result of an on-field injury. By that time, Mays, one of the first submarine style pitchers in baseball history, already had a reputation of brushing batters off the plate, even getting into an altercation with Ty Cobb in 1915. After a few close pitches, Cobb threw his bat towards Mays and the two began exchanging unpleasantries. When order was restored and Cobb stepped back into the batter's box, Mays proceeded to hit him on the wrist with a pitch.

In his one year with the Giants, his last before retiring at the age of 37, Mays started eight games, winning six of them while posting a 4.32 ERA.

# TONY LAZZERI

When most people think of the New Yankees of the 1920's and 1930's, the names Babe Ruth, Lou Gehrig, Joe DiMaggio, and Bill Dickey come to mind. You rarely hear the name Tony Lazzeri mentioned. But this Hall-of-Fame infielder played a big role in the success of those Yankee teams, starting with his rookie season in 1926 when he hit knocked out 18 home runs, drove in 117 and batted .275. Primarily used at second base, Lazzeri would go on to drive in over 100 runs six more times in his career, while supporting a career batting average of .292.

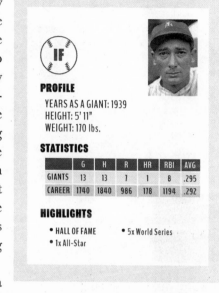

**PROFILE**
YEARS AS A GIANT: 1939
HEIGHT: 5' 11"
WEIGHT: 170 lbs.

**STATISTICS**

|  | G | H | R | HR | RBI | AVG |
|---|---|---|---|---|---|---|
| GIANTS | 13 | 13 | 7 | 1 | 8 | .295 |
| CAREER | 1740 | 1840 | 986 | 178 | 1194 | .292 |

**HIGHLIGHTS**
- HALL OF FAME
- 1x All-Star
- 5x World Series

On May 24, 1936, Lazzeri had a game for the record books when he hit two grand slam home runs, the first player to ever do that, and drove in 11 runs, which is still an American League record. Lazzeri is also one of only 14 Major League baseball players to hit for the natural cycle (single, double, triple, home run in order) and the only player to complete the natural cycle with a grand slam.

After the 1937 season, the Yankees released Lazzeri after he hit .244 in 126 games. The 33-year-old infielder then signed with the Chicago Cubs as a player-coach in 1938. Although he only played in 54 games where he hit .267 for Chicago, the Cubs won the National League pennant, only to lose to the Yankees in the 1938 World Series. Lazzeri went 0-2 against his old team. The Cubs released him after the World Series.

Lazzeri went on to sign with the Brooklyn Dodgers prior to the 1939 season, but was released on May 13 after batting .282 in 14 games with them. The next day, the Giants signed him to play third base. Lazzeri, a San Francisco native, went on to play 13 games for the Giants, getting 13 hits in 44 at bats for a .295 average, while knocking out one home run and driving in eight runs. He was released on June 7, 1939, and soon retired as a player at the age of 35, ending his 14-year career which saw him win five World Series championships.

Sadly, Lazzeri would die seven years later of a heart attack at the age of 42. He was voted into the Major League Baseball Hall-of-Fame in 1991.

# GABBY HARTNETT

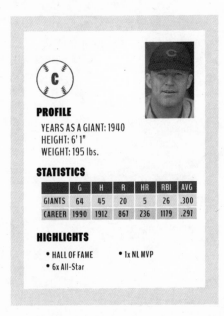

**PROFILE**

YEARS AS A GIANT: 1940
HEIGHT: 6' 1"
WEIGHT: 195 lbs.

**STATISTICS**

|  | G | H | R | HR | RBI | AVG |
|---|---|---|---|---|---|---|
| GIANTS | 64 | 45 | 20 | 5 | 26 | .300 |
| CAREER | 1990 | 1912 | 867 | 236 | 1179 | .297 |

**HIGHLIGHTS**

- HALL OF FAME
- 6x All-Star
- 1x NL MVP

During his playing days, Gabby Hartnett was considered the ultimate all-around catcher, performing equally well both offensively and defensively. Known for his strong and accurate throwing arm, he routinely led the National League's catchers in caught stealing percentage and was the first major league catcher to hit more than 20 home runs in a season, which he did in 1925 when he belted 24.

Harnett was an All-Star for the Chicago Cubs from 1933 through 1938, during which time he was named the 1935 National League MVP when he hit .344 while driving in 91 runs. In 1938, the 37-year-old catcher became the player/manager of the Cubs, and as a result his playing time on the field became reduced. In his final three seasons with the Cubs, Hartnett played in 88, 97, and 37 games.

After 19 years with the Cubs, Hartnett was dismissed by the Cubbies on November 13, 1940 following a disappointing 75-79 season. On December 10, he signed a contract with the New York Giants to be a player-coach. In 64 games with the Giants in 1941, Hartnett hit for a .300 average as a backup catcher to Harry Danning, while blasting five home runs and driving in 26. He played his final game on September 25, 1941, retiring as a player at the age of 40.

At the time of his retirement, Hartnett's 236 home runs, 1,179 RBIs, 1,912 hits, and 396 doubles were all records for catchers. Bill Dickey of the Yankees surpassed his records for most RBIs and hits in 1943, while his career home run record for catchers was broken by another Yankee, Yogi Berra in 1956. His career mark for doubles stood until 1983 when it was broken by Ted Simmons of the Milwaukee Brewers.

During the course of his career, Hartnett took part in some of the most memorable events in Major League Baseball history including Babe Ruth's Called Shot during the 1932 World Series.

# ERNIE LOMBARDI

Upon joining them as a rookie in 1932, Ernie Lombardi went on to play nine seasons with the Cincinnati Reds, winning a batting title and league MVP in 1938 before being purchased by the Boston Braves in February, 1942. The 34-year-old backstop then surprised everyone by hitting .330 and winning his second National League batting title in five years. No light achievement, as it would be 64 years before another catcher would capture a batting crown, when Joe Mauer of the Minnesota Twins did it in 2006. It would be 70 years before another National League catcher won the batting title, and ironically it would be a Giant: Buster Posey in 2012.

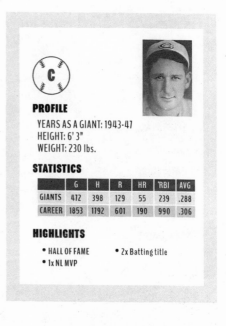

**PROFILE**
YEARS AS A GIANT: 1943-47
HEIGHT: 6' 3"
WEIGHT: 230 lbs.

**STATISTICS**

|        | G    | H    | R   | HR  | RBI | AVG  |
|--------|------|------|-----|-----|-----|------|
| GIANTS | 472  | 398  | 129 | 55  | 239 | .288 |
| CAREER | 1853 | 1792 | 601 | 190 | 990 | .306 |

**HIGHLIGHTS**
- HALL OF FAME
- 1x NL MVP
- 2x Batting title

After one season with the Braves, Boston traded Lombardi to the Giants on April 27, 1943 for a couple of rookies: outfielder Hugh Poland and infielder Connie Ryan. Lombardi, now 35, went on to have four decent seasons with the Giants, including his first year on the team when he hit .305 with 10 home runs and 51 RBIs while making his seventh and final All-Star team. His best season as a Giant, however, was in 1945 when he hit .307 with 19 home runs and 70 RBIs. After playing in only 48 games 1947, the Giants released the 39-year-old future Hall-of-Famer on September 20, 1947. Lombardi retired prior to the start of the next season.

Lombardi was posthumously inducted into the Bay Area Sports Hall of Fame in 1982 and the National Baseball Hall of Fame in 1986.

In case you're wondering, Hugh Poland began his career as a 33-year-old rookie with the Giants in 1942 and played in only four games before the trade, getting one hit in 12 at bats. Poland went on to play in 56 games over three years with Boston, hitting .182 with 0 hrs and 15 RBIs.

Twenty-two year old Connie Ryan played in only 11 games before the trade, knocking out five hits in 27 at bats. Ryan went on to play for seven years with Boston, averaging .247 with 20 home runs and 202 RBIs. His best season was 1947 when he drove in 69 runs and hit .265.

# VINCE DIMAGGIO

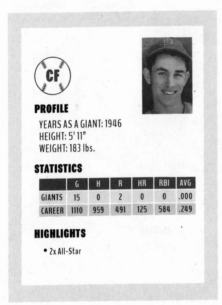

**PROFILE**
YEARS AS A GIANT: 1946
HEIGHT: 5' 11"
WEIGHT: 183 lbs.

**STATISTICS**

|  | G | H | R | HR | RBI | AVG |
|---|---|---|---|---|---|---|
| GIANTS | 15 | 0 | 2 | 0 | 0 | .000 |
| CAREER | 1110 | 959 | 491 | 125 | 584 | .249 |

**HIGHLIGHTS**
• 2x All-Star

"DiMaggio", a name forever embedded in Major League baseball history. Although not because of this DiMaggio, Vince DiMaggio, younger brother of the legendary Joe of the New York Yankees, who actually did have a respectable career with five MLB teams, most of them with the Pittsburgh Pirates. During his time as a Buc, DiMaggio was selected to the All-Star Game in 1943 and 1944. In the 1943 game, he collected a home run, triple, single, a pair of runs and one RBI over three at-bats.

On March 31, 1945, he was traded by the Pirates to the Philadelphia Phillies for Al Gerheauser. DiMaggio then went on to hit four grand slams for the Phillies in his one full season with the team. After playing six games for the Phillies in 1946, he was traded to the Giants on May 1, 1946 for catcher Clyde Kluttz. DiMaggio went on to finish the season with the Giants, playing in 15 games and going hitless in 25 at bats. The 33-year-old retired after the season, but not before ripping out 125 home runs, 584 RBIs and hitting for a .249 average during his 10-year career.

Klutz played in 78 games for the Giants over two seasons, and played until 1952 as a backup catcher for four teams. Ironically, one of them wasn't Philadelphia, as the Phillies shipped him to St. Louis the same day they got him from the Giants.

# JOE GARAGIOLA

In 1941, Joe Garagiola was signed by the St. Louis Cardinals organization at the ripe young age of 16. As a 20-year-old rookie in 1946, he played in his only World Series, batting 6-for-19 in five games, including a Game 4 where he went 4-for-5 with three RBIs. That was actually better than the great Ted Williams, who went only 5-for-25 in the same series, which sadly wound up being Williams' only World Series appearance.

Garagiola played in 676 games over nine seasons for four National League teams, only passing 100 in games in a season twice. His best year was in 1952 when he caught 118 games and hit .273

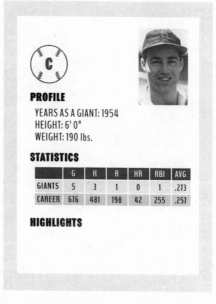

**PROFILE**
YEARS AS A GIANT: 1954
HEIGHT: 6' 0"
WEIGHT: 190 lbs.

**STATISTICS**

|  | G | H | R | HR | RBI | AVG |
|---|---|---|---|---|---|---|
| GIANTS | 5 | 3 | 1 | 0 | 1 | .273 |
| CAREER | 676 | 481 | 198 | 42 | 255 | .257 |

**HIGHLIGHTS**

with eight home runs and 54 RBIs. The last of the four teams be played for was the Giants, who claimed him off of waivers on September 8, 1954 from the Chicago Cubs to primarily help the team finish the season. Garagiola played five games for the Giants, getting three hits in 11 at-bats with one RBI, before retiring after the season at the ripe old age of 28.

# JACKIE ROBINSON

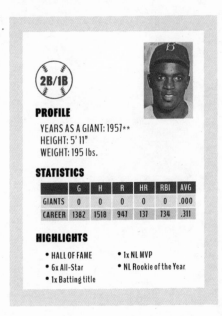

**2B/1B**

**PROFILE**
YEARS AS A GIANT: 1957**
HEIGHT: 5' 11"
WEIGHT: 195 lbs.

**STATISTICS**

| | G | H | R | HR | RBI | AVG |
|---|---|---|---|---|---|---|
| GIANTS | 0 | 0 | 0 | 0 | 0 | .000 |
| CAREER | 1382 | 1518 | 947 | 137 | 734 | .311 |

**HIGHLIGHTS**

- HALL OF FAME
- 6x All-Star
- 1x Batting title
- 1x NL MVP
- NL Rookie of the Year

Jackie Robinson, a Giant? Wonder how many people did a double take when they saw that! Well, to be honest, an asterisk has to be included here. Yes, Robinson was actually traded to the Giants after the 1956 season on December 13, but he never played a game for them.

By 1956, the 37-year-old Robinson's productivity was beginning to fall off, partly due to effects from diabetes. After playing in only 107 and 117 games the prior two seasons and hitting career low averages of .256 and .275, the 37-year-old 10-year veteran, unbeknownst to the Dodgers, had already decided to retire from baseball after the 1956 season. In fact, Robinson had already agreed with the President of *Chock full o'Nuts*, an east coast chain of coffee shops around since 1926, to quit baseball and become an executive with the company. Unaware of this, however, the Dodgers traded Robinson to the Giants for pitcher Dick Littlefield and $35,000 cash on December 13, 1956. The trade, however, was never completed, as Robinson refused to report and both players were returned to their respective teams. Robinson did indeed officially retire three weeks later on January 5, 1957.

During his groundbreaking career with the Dodgers, Robinson averaged .311 while hitting 137 home runs and driving in 734 RBIs. A six-time All-Star, Robinson was the 1947 Rookie-of-the-Year, and 1949 National League Batting Champion and League MVP.

After his trade for Robinson fell through, the Giants traded Littlefield four months later along with right fielder Bob Lennon to the Chicago Cubs for utility man Ray Jablonski and catcher Ray Katt.

Katt batted .232 in 336 games. King hit .214 in 34 games for the Giants before being released after the 1958 season.

# HANK SAUER

A two-time All-Star, Hank Sauer was a feared slugger for the Cubs in the early 1950s, hitting over 30 home runs in six seasons, and belting a career-high 41 in 1954. His most productive season came in 1952, when he led the National League with 37 home runs and 121 RBIs, and was named the National League's Most Valuable Player.

In 1955, Sauer tried to hold out for a bigger contract with the Cubs, but Chicago decided to trade the 38-year-old to the St. Louis Cardinals instead, where he became the roommate of Stan Musial. When the Cardinals released him after the 1956 season, the Giants swooped in

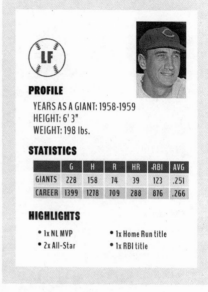

**PROFILE**
YEARS AS A GIANT: 1958-1959
HEIGHT: 6' 3"
WEIGHT: 198 lbs.

**STATISTICS**

|  | G | H | R | HR | RBI | AVG |
|---|---|---|---|---|---|---|
| GIANTS | 228 | 158 | 74 | 39 | 123 | .251 |
| CAREER | 1399 | 1278 | 709 | 288 | 876 | .266 |

**HIGHLIGHTS**

- 1x NL MVP
- 2x All-Star
- 1x Home Run title
- 1x RBI title

and signed the slugger on October 26, 1956. Sauer played the next three seasons with the Giants, one in New York and two in San Francisco, playing in 228 games, batting .251 while hitting 39 home runs and 123 RBIs. Sauer's best season was his first and only as a New York Giant, when he hit 26 home runs, drove in 76 and batted .259 in 127 games. He was rewarded by being voted the National League Comeback Player of the Year award that year.

Once in San Francisco, his playing time began to diminish as his spot on the team changed into a reserve role, and he played in only 88 and 13 games during his final two years. The Giants released the 42-year-old Sauer on August 25, 1959 as a player, but was soon signed on as a hitting coach. After his playing days were over, Sauer served in several different capacities with the Giants for the next 35 years, including as a hitting instructor, scout, and even running the teams Farm system and Arizona instructional league squad for a period of time.

# DUKE SNIDER

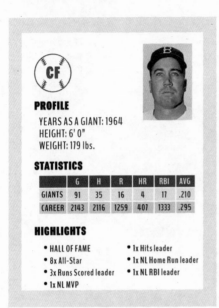

**PROFILE**
YEARS AS A GIANT: 1964
HEIGHT: 6' 0"
WEIGHT: 179 lbs.

**STATISTICS**

|  | G | H | R | HR | RBI | AVG |
|---|---|---|---|---|---|---|
| GIANTS | 91 | 35 | 16 | 4 | 17 | .210 |
| CAREER | 2143 | 2116 | 1259 | 407 | 1333 | .295 |

**HIGHLIGHTS**

- HALL OF FAME
- 8x All-Star
- 3x Runs Scored leader
- 1x NL MVP
- 1x Hits leader
- 1x NL Home Run leader
- 1x NL RBI leader

Duke Snider is another player that many fans might find surprising played for the Giants. Snider, of course became a legend during his years as a Brooklyn and Los Angeles Dodger from 1947 through 1962. He won the National League MVP in 1955 when he led the league with 136 RBIs. He won the World Series with the Dodgers in 1955 and 1959.

Injuries and age would eventually play a role in reducing Snider to part-time status by 1961, where he would only play in 85 games that year, and 80 in 1962. Then on April 1, 1963, the 35-year-old returned to New York after the Dodgers sold him to the New York Mets. The Mets, in only their second season of existence, were still trying to find their legs, and suffered through a 51-111 regular season. That was enough for Snider, as after one season with the Mets, in which he played in 129 games, hit 14 home runs, drove in 45 runs and posted a .243 average, he asked to be traded to a contending team.

As a result, Snider returned to the west coast after being sold to the San Francisco Giants on Opening Day on April 14, 1964. Interestingly, the number "4", which Snider had worn his entire career, had also been worn by Mel Ott and retired by the Giants. So Snider settled on the number 28 instead. Snider played the entire 1964 season with the Giants, playing all three outfield positions, and in 91 games batted .210 with four home runs and 17 RBIs. He had no triples for the first and only time in his career. Although he had the opportunity to be in the same lineup as old rivals Willie Mays and Willie McCovey, the Giants finished fourth that season, posting a 90-72 record, three games behind the National League champion St. Louis Cardinals.

Snider retired at the end of the 1964 season at the age of 37 after the Giants released him on October 6, 1964. He was voted into the Major League Baseball Hall of Fame in 1980.

# WARREN SPAHN

With all due respect to Sandy Koufax, Steve Carlton, Lefty Grove, Carl Hubbell, Randy Johnson and a few others, Warren Spahn has to be regarded as the greatest all-around left-handed pitcher in Major League Baseball history. Just take a look at these facts: pitched in 21 seasons; won 363 games; won three ERA titles; eight win titles; four strikeout titles; won 20 games 13 times; hit 35 career home runs; played in 17 All-Star games; won six pitcher of the year titles and one Cy Young.

But what really makes Spahn remarkable is what he did after the age of 35. From the age of 35 through 40, he won 20 or more games each season...

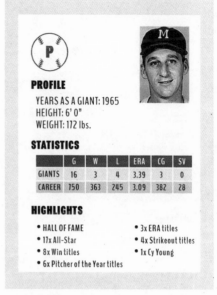

**PROFILE**
YEARS AS A GIANT: 1965
HEIGHT: 6' 0"
WEIGHT: 172 lbs.

**STATISTICS**

|  | G | W | L | ERA | CG | SV |
|---|---|---|---|---|---|---|
| GIANTS | 16 | 3 | 4 | 3.39 | 3 | 0 |
| CAREER | 750 | 363 | 245 | 3.09 | 382 | 28 |

**HIGHLIGHTS**

- HALL OF FAME
- 17x All-Star
- 8x Win titles
- 6x Pitcher of the Year titles
- 3x ERA titles
- 4x Strikeout titles
- 1x Cy Young

that's six in a row! He won 23 games at the age of 42, and pitched a complete 15 inning, 201 pitch game that year in which he lost to the Giants and Juan Marichal, 1-0. He pitched his first no-hitter at the age of 39, and followed that up the following year by pitching another one at age 40. Of the 35 career home runs he hit, nine were after the age 40, including four in 1961 at the age of 40. Simply mind-boggling, and something very unlikely to be seen again.

Following the 1964 season however, at the age of 44, the gas tank was finally starting to run dry for Spahn. Although, incredibly, he was able to make 38 starts that season, he went 6-13 with a 5.29 ERA, the lowest win total and highest ERA in his entire career up to that point. So after 25 years with the franchise, Spahn was sold by the Atlanta Braves to the New York Mets on November 23, 1964.

After going 4-12 in 20 starts, the Mets put Spahn on waivers on July 17, 1965. He immediately signed with the Giants who were battling the rival Dodgers for the National League pennant, with the hope that Spahn would give them an added edge, and perhaps give the lefty one last chance at winning his second World Series title.

Alas, that was not meant to be however, as Spahn went 3-4 in 16 starts for San Francisco. Although the Giants finished a superb 95-67 in 1965, it would be two games behind the league champion Dodgers. That season would be the last in his remarkable 21 year major league career, as the Giants would release him on October 15, 1965. He would retire soon after.

# DICK GROAT

**PROFILE**

YEARS AS A GIANT: 1967
HEIGHT: 5' 11"
WEIGHT: 180 lbs.

**STATISTICS**

| | G | H | R | HR | RBI | AVG |
|---|---|---|---|---|---|---|
| GIANTS | 34 | 12 | 4 | 0 | 4 | .171 |
| CAREER | 1929 | 2138 | 829 | 39 | 101 | .286 |

**HIGHLIGHTS**

• 1x NL MVP
• 5x All-Star

The year 1952 is one that Dick Groat would never forget. Not only was he signed as an amateur by the Pittsburgh Pirates that year, he was the third overall pick in the 1952 NBA Draft by the Fort Wayne Pistons of the National Basketball Association.

Groat played college basketball for Duke University, and was an All-American twice in 1951 and 1952. He was the UPI National Player of the Year in 1952 after setting an NCAA record with 839 points. During that season, he scored 48 points against North Carolina, still the most ever scored against the Tar Heels.

Groat played one season in the NBA, averaging 11.9 points, 3.3 rebounds, and 2.7 assists in 26 games before his basketball career was cut short by military service. Once his enlistment time was up, he returned to the Pirates, but chose not to play basketball.

A five-time National League All-Star, Groat's prime came in the early sixties when he won the National League MVP award for 1960 as he lead the league in hitting with a .325 average. His best year statistically was actually three years later when he drove in 70 runs and hit .319 for the 1963 St. Louis Cardinals, while knocking out over 200 hits for the only time in his career. Groat finished second in the National League MVP voting that season. Groat had been traded to the Cardinals for two pitchers after the prior season as the Pirates were looking to bolster their pitching staff.

After hitting .254 in 1965 for the Cardinals, the 34-year-old Groat was traded to the Philadelphia Phillies in a six-player deal. He batted .265 for the 1966 Phillies before his contract was sold to the Giants on June 22, 1967 missing two months with an ankle injury. Groat did finish the year with San Francisco, batting .171 in 34 games, but retired at the end of the season, his 14th, at the age of 36.

Groat is one of 13 athletes who played in both the National Basketball Association and Major League Baseball.

# DAN QUISENBERRY

In the 1980's, Dan Quisenberry, Bruce Sutter, and a few others officially ushered in the era of the reliever and closer following their predecessors Rich Gossage and Rollie Fingers a decade earlier. Quisenberry's 45 saves in 1983 was briefly a single-season record (tied in 1984 by Bruce Sutter and broken in 1986 by Dave Righetti), and he was the first pitcher in major league history to save more than 40 games in a season twice in his career. He won a World Series with the Royals in 1985 and was the winning pitcher of Game 6.

In 1983, the Royals signed Quisenberry to a lifetime contract, similar to that

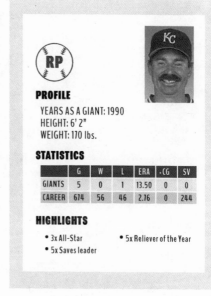

**PROFILE**
YEARS AS A GIANT: 1990
HEIGHT: 6' 2"
WEIGHT: 170 lbs.

**STATISTICS**

|  | G | W | L | ERA | -CG | SV |
|---|---|---|---|---|---|---|
| GIANTS | 5 | 0 | 1 | 13.50 | 0 | 0 |
| CAREER | 674 | 56 | 46 | 2.76 | 0 | 244 |

**HIGHLIGHTS**
- 3x All-Star
- 5x Reliever of the Year
- 5x Saves leader

of teammate George Brett. However, a rocky start in 1988 led to Quisenberry's relegation to middle relief and mop-up duty. Shortly before the All-Star break that year, he was released by the Royals. Ten days later the St. Louis Cardinals, managed by ex-Royals manager Whitey Herzog, signed Quisenberry as a free agent.

After pitching for a year and a half in St. Louis, Quisenberry signed to play with the San Francisco Giants as a free agent on January 28, 1990. He tore his rotator cuff just five appearances and 6.2 innings into the 1990 season, and was faced with serious injury for the first time in his career. As a result, Quisenberry decided to retire from baseball at the age of 37 after 12 seasons in the majors. But not before winning five Reliever of the Year awards and participating in three All-Star games.

In January 1998, Quisenberry was diagnosed with grade IV astrocytoma, a highly malignant form of brain cancer, and tragically died at age 45 in September 1998 in Kansas.

# JOE CARTER

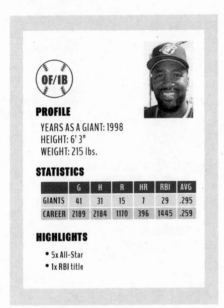

**OF/1B**

**PROFILE**
YEARS AS A GIANT: 1998
HEIGHT: 6' 3"
WEIGHT: 215 lbs.

**STATISTICS**

|  | G | H | R | HR | RBI | AVG |
|---|---|---|---|---|---|---|
| GIANTS | 41 | 31 | 15 | 7 | 29 | .295 |
| CAREER | 2189 | 2184 | 1170 | 396 | 1445 | .259 |

**HIGHLIGHTS**

• 5x All-Star
• 1x RBI title

Although he had several very productive seasons with the Cleveland Indians and San Diego Padres early in his career, it wasn't until 1992 and 1993 that Joe Carter became a household name. Prior to the 1991 season, Carter was involved in a trade that sent him and Roberto Alomar from the Padres to the Toronto Blue Jays for two of their stars, Fred McGriff and Tony Hernandez. In 1992, Carter helped the Blue Jays win their first World Series championship, the first ever won by a Canadian-based team. Carter hit two home runs in the series.

In 1993, the Blue Jays reached the World Series again and faced the Philadelphia Phillies. In Game 6, with the Blue Jays leading three games to two, Carter came to bat with one out in the bottom of the ninth inning with the Blue Jays trailing 6–5. With Rickey Henderson and Paul Molitor on base, Carter ripped a three-run walk-off home run off Phillies pitcher Mitch Williams to win the World Series, only the second time a Series has ended on a home run. Bill Mazeroski of the Pittsburgh Pirates did it 33 years earlier to defeat the New York Yankees.

Carter went on to play four more seasons with the Blue Jays, becoming an All-Star twice. But after the 1997 season, the 38-year-old became a free agent and subsequently signed with the Baltimore Orioles. After spending half the season with the Orioles where he hit .247 with 11 home runs and 34 RBIs, Baltimore traded Carter to the Giants on July 23, 1998 for minor leaguer pitcher Darin Blood. Carter finished the season with the Giants, playing in 41 games while hitting .295 with seven home runs and 29 RBIs before calling it a career. Blood never pitched at the Major League level.

# ERIC DAVIS

Most baseball fans are aware of what Eric Davis did in his first eight years as a Cincinnati Red: great defense, two-time All-Star, first player to hit 30 home runs and steal 50 bases, the first to hit three grand slam home runs in one month, and World Series champion in 1990.

But what Davis did in the latter part of his career is really what really was amazing and inspirational. After surgery for a lacerated kidney he had suffered during game 4 of the 1990 World Series, as well as a bad knee he had hurt earlier that season, injuries began to slowly take over Davis's career. In fact, he was only able to play in over 100 games in a season

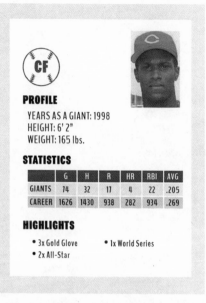

## PROFILE
YEARS AS A GIANT: 1998
HEIGHT: 6' 2"
WEIGHT: 165 lbs.

## STATISTICS

|        | G    | H    | R   | HR  | RBI | AVG  |
|--------|------|------|-----|-----|-----|------|
| GIANTS | 74   | 32   | 11  | 4   | 22  | .205 |
| CAREER | 1626 | 1430 | 938 | 282 | 934 | .269 |

## HIGHLIGHTS

- 3x Gold Glove
- 2x All-Star
- 1x World Series

three times in the next 11 years. Fatigue and a hamstring injury, broken collar-bone and a shoulder injury limited Davis to 89 and 76 games in 1990 and 1991. Following short stints with the Dodgers and Tigers from 1992-1994 where he only played in a total of 191 games, Davis actually decided to retire after the 1994 season when he had to undergo surgery because of a herniated disc in his neck.

But after sitting out 1995, a healthier, hungry Davis decided to give it another go and rejoined the Reds, where he had a solid 1996 season by hitting .287, with 26 home runs and 83 RBIs. The Reds, however, decided not to bring Davis back, and he subsequently signed with the Baltimore Orioles. He started the 1997 season well before being set back by a stomach ailment in May of that season that would later be diagnosed as colon cancer. After having a portion of his colon removed and following a series of chemotherapy treatments, Davis remarkably rejoined the Orioles in time for the playoffs, and even hit a game winning home run in the American League Championship series against Cleveland, which Baltimore would eventually lose.

The Orioles brought Davis back in 1998 where he had one of his best years in his career, playing in 131 games, hitting .327 while knocking out 28 home runs and driving in 89. After the season, he signed a two-year deal with the St. Louis Cardinals, but only played 58 games in 1999 because of a torn rotator cuff. After appearing in 92 games with the Cards in 2000, Davis signed with the Giants in 2001 and played in 74 games that year. After batting only .205 with four home runs and 22 RBIs, Davis retired for good at the age of 39, ending his 17-year career.

# RANDY JOHNSON

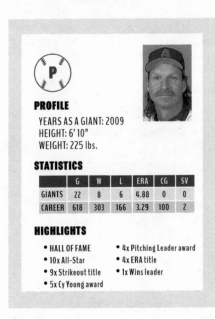

**PROFILE**
YEARS AS A GIANT: 2009
HEIGHT: 6' 10"
WEIGHT: 225 lbs.

**STATISTICS**

|  | G | W | L | ERA | CG | SV |
|---|---|---|---|---|---|---|
| GIANTS | 22 | 8 | 6 | 4.88 | 0 | 0 |
| CAREER | 618 | 303 | 166 | 3.29 | 100 | 2 |

**HIGHLIGHTS**

- HALL OF FAME
- 10x All-Star
- 9x Strikeout title
- 5x Cy Young award
- 4x Pitching Leader award
- 4x ERA title
- 1x Wins leader

After logging an 11–10 record and 3.91 ERA during a 2008 season which saw Randy Johnson record his 100th career complete game, the Arizona Diamondbacks waived the 45-year-old free agent on November 13, 2008, just five wins short of the magical 300 number.

On December 26, 2008, the 6'10" Johnson, aptly nicknamed "the Big Unit", signed a one-year deal with the Giants in his quest to become only the twenty-fourth pitcher in Major League Baseball history to reach 300 wins. And on June 4, 2009, he did just that, beating the Washington Nationals 5-1 at Nationals Park in Washington, D.C.

Less than two months later, however, Johnson was placed on the 60-day disabled list with a torn rotator cuff in his throwing shoulder. On September 16, Johnson was activated and assigned to the Giants bullpen, and three days later made his first relief appearance in four years, facing three batters in a game versus the Los Angeles Dodgers. Four months after the season ended, on January 5, 2010, Johnson announced his retirement from professional baseball. During his single season with the Giants, Johnson went 8-6 with a 4.88 ERA in 22 games, striking out 86 hitters in 96 innings.

His 303 career victories rank as the fifth-most by a left-hander in Major League Baseball history, while his 4,875 strikeouts place him second all-time behind Nolan Ryan and are the most by a left-hander. On May 18, 2004, at the age of forty, Johnson became the oldest pitcher in Major League Baseball history to throw a perfect game. He is also one of eighteen pitchers in history to record a win against all 30 franchises.

# OTHER PLAYERS OF NOTE

In the early days of baseball, it was commonplace to see a player with a colorful nickname that matched their personality or skill set. For whatever the reason, these catchy nicknames began disappearing in the 1940's and were almost non-existent from the 1950's onward. But here are a few of the most noteworthy who played for the Giants, and the first year they played for the team.

* Dasher Troy - 2B - 1883
* Jocko Fields - IF - 1892
* General Stafford - IF/OF - 1893
* King Kelly - C- 1893
* Oyster Burns - OF - 1895
* Dad Clark - P - 1897
* Pink Hawley - P - 1900
* Dummy Taylor - P - 1900
* Hook Wiltse - P - 1904
* Bull Durham - P - 1908
* Moose McCormick - OF - 1909
* Chief Meyers - C- 1909
* Ferdie Schupp - P - 1914
* High Pockets Kelly - OF/IF - 1915
* Sailor Stroud - P - 1915
* Slim Sallee - P - 1918
* Jigger Statz - OF - 1920
* Pug Griffin - OF – 1920
* Rosy Ryan - P - 1920
* Goldie Rapp - 3B - 1921

* Irish Meusel - LF - 1921
* Cozy Dolan - OF/IF - 1922
* Dinty Gearin - P - 1923
* Bullet Joe Bush - P - 1927
* Burleigh Grimes - P - 1927
* Lefty O'Doul - LF/P - 1928
* Chick Fullis - OF - 1930
* Tiny Chaplin - P - 1930
* Hughie Critz - 2B - 1932
* Tip Tobin - IN/OF - 1932
* Hi Bell - P - 1932
* Blondy Ryan - SS - 1933
* Kiddo Davis - OF - 1933
* Homer Peel - OF - 1933
* Skeeter Scalzi - SS - 1939
* Ace Adams - P - 1941
* Goody Rosen - OF - 1946
* Hooks Iott - P - 1947
* Tookie Gilbert - 1B - 1950
* Spider Jorgensen - 3B - 1950

# THE GIANTS BY THE NUMBERS

The following shows where the Giants franchise ranks among Major League Baseball teams in a variety of categories as of 2019, going back to 1876 when baseball first began.

## GAMES

| Rk | FRANCHISE | FROM | TO | G ▼ |
|---|---|---|---|---|
| 1 | CHICAGO CUBS | 1876 | 2018 | 21,385 |
| 2 | ATLANTA BRAVES | 1876 | 2018 | 21,348 |
| 3 | ST. LOUIS CARDINALS | 1882 | 2018 | 20,971 |
| 4 | CINCINNATI REDS | 1882 | 2018 | 20,969 |
| 5 | PITTSBURGH PIRATES | 1882 | 2018 | 20,928 |
| 6 | SAN FRANCISCO GIANTS | 1883 | 2018 | 20,853 |

## WINS

| Rk | FRANCHISE | FROM | TO | W ▼ |
|---|---|---|---|---|
| 1 | SAN FRANCISCO GIANTS | 1883 | 2018 | 11,088 |
| 2 | CHICAGO CUBS | 1876 | 2018 | 10,898 |
| 3 | LOS ANGELES DODGERS | 1884 | 2018 | 10,868 |
| 4 | ST. LOUIS CARDINALS | 1882 | 2018 | 10,827 |
| 5 | ATLANTA BRAVES | 1876 | 2018 | 10,600 |

## WINNING PERCENTAGE

| Rk | FRANCHISE | FROM | TO | W-L%▼ |
|---|---|---|---|---|
| 1 | NEW YORK YANKEES | 1903 | 2018 | .569 |
| 2 | SAN FRANCISCO GIANTS | 1883 | 2018 | .536 |
| 3 | LOS ANGELES DODGERS | 1884 | 2018 | .527 |
| 4 | ST. LOUIS CARDINALS | 1882 | 2018 | .520 |
| 5 | BOSTON RED SOX | 1901 | 2018 | .519 |

## RUNS

| Rk | FRANCHISE | FROM | TO | R ▼ |
|---|---|---|---|---|
| 1 | CHICAGO CUBS | 1876 | 2018 | 98,434 |
| 2 | SAN FRANCISCO GIANTS | 1883 | 2018 | 96,590 |
| 3 | ST. LOUIS CARDINALS | 1882 | 2018 | 96,242 |
| 4 | ATLANTA BRAVES | 1876 | 2018 | 94,892 |
| 5 | CINCINNATI REDS | 1882 | 2018 | 94,139 |

## HITS

| Rk | FRANCHISE | FROM | TO | H ▼ |
|---|---|---|---|---|
| 1 | CHICAGO CUBS | 1876 | 2018 | 192,394 |
| 2 | ST. LOUIS CARDINALS | 1882 | 2018 | 191,701 |
| 3 | ATLANTA BRAVES | 1876 | 2018 | 190,022 |
| 4 | PITTSBURGH PIRATES | 1882 | 2018 | 189,657 |
| 5 | SAN FRANCISCO GIANTS | 1883 | 2018 | 188,007 |

## HOME RUNS

| Rk | FRANCHISE | FROM | TO | HR▼ |
|---|---|---|---|---|
| 1 | NEW YORK YANKEES | 1903 | 2018 | 15,909 |
| 2 | SAN FRANCISCO GIANTS | 1883 | 2018 | 14,515 |
| 3 | CHICAGO CUBS | 1876 | 2018 | 14,119 |
| 4 | DETROIT TIGERS | 1901 | 2018 | 13,693 |
| 5 | ATLANTA BRAVES | 1876 | 2018 | 13,651 |

## BATTING AVERAGE

| Rk | FRANCHISE | FROM | TO | BA▼ |
|---|---|---|---|---|
| 1 | COLORADO ROCKIES | 1993 | 2018 | .274 |
| 2 | BOSTON RED SOX | 1901 | 2018 | .267 |
| 3 | ST. LOUIS CARDINALS | 1882 | 2018 | .266 |
| 4 | CLEVELAND INDIANS | 1901 | 2018 | .266 |
| 5 | NEW YORK YANKEES | 1903 | 2018 | .266 |
| 6 | DETROIT TIGERS | 1901 | 2018 | .265 |
| 7 | PITTSBURGH PIRATES | 1882 | 2018 | .264 |
| 8 | SAN FRANCISCO GIANTS | 1883 | 2018 | .264 |

## ERA

| Rk | FRANCHISE | FROM | TO | ERA▼ |
|---|---|---|---|---|
| 1 | LOS ANGELES DODGERS | 1884 | 2018 | 3.53 |
| 2 | SAN FRANCISCO GIANTS | 1883 | 2018 | 3.57 |
| 3 | NEW YORK YANKEES | 1903 | 2018 | 3.65 |
| 4 | ATLANTA BRAVES | 1876 | 2018 | 3.66 |
| 5 | ST. LOUIS CARDINALS | 1882 | 2018 | 3.67 |

## WORLD SERIES

| Rk | FRANCHISE | FROM | TO | WS▼ |
|---|---|---|---|---|
| 1 | NEW YORK YANKEES | 1903 | 2018 | 27 |
| 2 | ST. LOUIS CARDINALS | 1882 | 2018 | 11 |
| 3 | BOSTON RED SOX | 1901 | 2018 | 9 |
| 4 | OAKLAND ATHLETICS | 1901 | 2018 | 9 |
| 5 | SAN FRANCISCO GIANTS | 1883 | 2018 | 8 |

## HALL OF FAMERS

| Rk | FRANCHISE | FROM | TO | HOF#▼ |
|---|---|---|---|---|
| 1 | SAN FRANCISCO GIANTS | 1883 | 2018 | 57 |
| 2 | ATLANTA BRAVES | 1876 | 2018 | 52 |
| 3 | LOS ANGELES DODGERS | 1884 | 2018 | 50 |
| 4 | NEW YORK YANKEES | 1903 | 2018 | 45 |
| 5 | ST. LOUIS CARDINALS | 1882 | 2018 | 45 |

Source: *"Baseball Reference"*: https://www.baseball-reference.com/

# THE GIANTS – A TIMELINE

The following outlines some of the milestones of the New York/San Francisco Giants franchise, beginning with their birth in 1883 as the New York Gothams. Source: https://www.mlb.com/giants/history

## THE 1800'S

**1883:** John B. Day and Jim Mutrie, owners of the American Association's New York Metropolitans, form a National League team called the New York Gothams.

**1885:** Jim Mutrie becomes the manager of the Gothams, and he and John Day move some of the star players from the pennant-winning Metropolitans over to the National League franchise. The Gothams become known as the Giants during the season. On May 1, they play their first game at the Polo Grounds, a field once used for polo matches at 110th Street and Sixth Avenue.

**1888:** After two seasons of .550-plus records that nevertheless result in finishing more than 10 games back, the Giants capture their first National League pennant and then defeat the American Association's St. Louis Browns to claim their first world championship.

Tim Keefe set a franchise record by reeling off 19 straight victories as part of a 35-12 season. He topped the league in wins, ERA (1.74) and strikeouts (335), while teammate Mickey Welch contributed another 26 wins. Mike Tiernan also made franchise history by becoming the first Giant to hit for the cycle.

# 1900 - 1940

**1900:** 19-year-old Christy Mathewson begins his illustrious career on July 17. He would go on to pitch 17 seasons for the Giants, winning 30+ games in a season four times, including 37 in 1908. He also posted a career 2.13 ERA with 2,507 strikeouts. He would be part of the inaugural MLB Hall of Fame (Hall of Fame) class in 1939.

**1901:** Christy Mathewson tosses a no-hitter, one of two in his Hall of Fame career, against the St. Louis Cardinals.

**1902:** Suffering the most miserable finish in the team's 20-year history (48-88, 53 1/2 games back), New York still makes a move that would prove to be one of the most significant ever: signing John McGraw as player-manager.

**1904:** After crushing the rest of the league with a franchise-best 106 victories to capture the National League title, the Giants decline to participate in the newly created World Series because manager John McGraw and owner John Brush consider the American League a minor league.

Satisfied with the adoption of certain postseason rules, the Giants agree to play in the World Series after successfully defending their National League championship. Christy Mathewson authors one of the greatest pitching performances in history, tallying three shutout victories in New York's four-games-to-one triumph over the Philadelphia Athletics for the Giants' first World Series title.

**1916:** Giants post a Major League record 26 game winning streak.

**1917:** The Giants appear in, and lose, their fourth straight World Series, this time to the Chicago White Sox.

**1920-1924:** The Giants win four straight National League pennants, resulting in four straight World Series appearances and two World Series titles (1921, 1922).

**1926:** Mel Ott makes his playing debut with the Giants on April 27 at the ripe old age of 17. He would play for the next 22 years as a Giant, retiring in 1947 with 511 home runs and a .304 batting average. He would be inducted into the MLB Hall of Fame in 1951.

**1928:** Carl Hubbell makes his pitching debut with the Giants on July 28. He would pitch his entire career for the Giants, retiring in 1943 with 253 wins and a lifetime 2.98 ERA. He would be inducted into the MLB Hall of Fame in 1947.

**1930:** The Giants .319 team batting average sets a Major League baseball record, while Bill Terry establishes a franchise record with a .401 average, making him the last National Leaguer to hit .400 or better.

**1936-1937:** Giants lose back-to-back World Series to the New York Yankees.

# 1941 - 1960

**1943:** Giants acquire future Hall-of-Famer "Big Cat" Johnny Mize.

**1944:** Carl Hubbell retires after 1943 season.

**1948:** Giants name recently fired Brooklyn Dodger manager Leo "the lip" Durocher as manager.

**1949:** On July 8, Monte Irvin and Hank Thompson become the first black players to play for the Giants.

**1951:** Willie Mays made his debut after hitting .477 in the minors, but went 0-for-12 to start his inaugural Major League season before crushing a Warren Spahn pitch completely out of the Polo Grounds. That would be the first of 20 long balls he would hit in his rookie season.

After trailing the Dodgers by 13 1/2 games on Aug. 11, manager Leo Durocher's troops rattled off 16 straight victories and won 37 of their final 44 regular-season contests to force a tie with Brooklyn. The Giants would win the third game of the three game playoff when Bobby Thompson hit his famous "The Miracle of Coogan's Bluff," homer off of Dodger reliever Ralph Branca.

**1954:** The Giants would go on to sweep the Cleveland Indians in four games to register their first World Series since 1933 in an upset over the highly touted American League champion, winners of 111 games. I would be the franchise's last World Series championship until 2010.

**1957:** On August 19, Giants owner Horace Stoneham announced that the Giants would be moving to the Bay Area for the 1958 season after previously considering Minnesota. However, San Francisco mayor George Christopher and Dodgers owner Walter O'Malley's convinced Stoneham that the Giants and Dodgers should move together to the West Coast.

**1958:** On April 15, the Giants began their tenure in San Francisco as Ruben Gomez shut out the Dodgers 8-0 while rookie first baseman from Puerto Rico hit a home run in his second Major League at-bat.

**1959:** Future Hall of Famer Willie McCovey goes 4-for-4 in his Major League debut en route to Rookie of the Year honors.

**1960:** On April 12, the Giants take the field for the first time at Candlestick Park.

# 1961 - 1980

**1961:** Willie Mays smacks four home runs in one game at Milwaukee County Stadium.

**1962:** In what was perhaps the greatest pitching duel in Major League baseball history, 25-year-old Juan Marichal and 42-year-old Warren Spahn battled it out on July 2 at Candlestick Park. The two future Hall-of-Famers would match each other pitch for pitch for 16 scoreless innings until a Willie Mays homer won the game for the Giants. Neither pitcher would concede to being replaced by a reliever, although both managers tried. After Giants manager Alvin Dark suggested that Marichal give way to the bullpen after the 9th inning, Marchical replied, "A 42-year-old man is still pitching. I can't come out."

The Giants and Dodgers finished the regular season with identical records of 101-61, forcing another three game playoff just like 10 years earlier. Once again, the Giants defeat the Dodgers in the third and deciding game. And just like 10 years earlier, the Giants go on to lose the World Series to the New York Yankees.

**1963:** On September 10, Jesus, Matty and Felipe Alou comprise the first all-brother outfield in Major League history.

**1964:** On September 1st, Masanori Murakami becomes the 1st Japanese player to play in the Major Leagues.

**1965:** On September 13, Willie Mays blasted his 500th home run to join Babe Ruth, Jimmie Foxx, Ted Williams and Mel Ott as a member of the 500 home run club.

**1968:** On September 17, Gaylord Perry tossed his only career no-hitter in a 1-0 duel victory over Bob Gibson and the St. Louis Cardinals. The celebration didn't last long, however, as on the very next day the Cardinals' Ray Washburn stunned the Giants by pitching a no-hitter of his own.

**1969:** September 22, Willie Mays 600th career home run comes in a pinch-hit role with the game tied in the 7th inning en route to a victory over the Padres.

**1973:** Willie Mays traded to Mets.

Although finishing 11 games out of first, the Giants have three young players garner national recognition: Bobby Bonds, who misses becoming baseball's first 40-40 man by one home run, is named The Sporting News' Player of the Year; southpaw Ron Bryant is named Pitcher of the Year after winning 24 games (still the most ever by a San Francisco lefty); outfielder Gary Matthews wins Rookie of the Year honors.

On October 25, the Giants traded 35-year-old Willie McCovey to the San Diego Padres with Bernie Williams for pitcher Mike Caldwell.

On December 7, 35-year-old Juan Marichal is sold to the Boston Red Sox. He would go on to win five games for the Red Sox in 11 starts before being released at the end of the 1974 season. On March 15, 1975, Marichal signed with the Dodgers where he would make two starts in 1975 before retiring.

**1975:** On August 24, pitcher Ed Halicki tosses a no-hitter.

Pitcher John Montefusco wins Rookie of the Year.

Bob Lurie saves the Giants from a possible move to Toronto by heading a group that buys the team and keeps it in San Francisco.

**1976:** On September 29, John Montefusco came within one pitch of a perfect game, hurling a 9-0 no-hitter against the Atlanta Braves.

**1977:** On January 6, Willie McCovey returns to the Giants as a free agent and wins the Comeback Player of the Year Award with a team-best 28 home runs at the age of 39.

**1978:** On June 30th, Willie McCovey belts his 500th career home run in Atlanta, making him the 12th player at the time to reach the 500 home run milestone.

**1980:** July 6, Willie McCovey takes his final at bat before 46,244 adoring fans, delivering a sac fly off Rick Sutcliffe to cap his four-decade, Hall of Fame career.

# 1981 - 2014:

**1981:** Frank Robinson becomes the first black manager in the National League when he is named to head the Giants.

**1985:** The Giants falter to the only 100-loss season in their history. Reliever Scott Garrelts leads the staff with a measly nine wins, and the team bats a league-worst .233.

**1986:** Giants begin their turnaround by signing Manager Roger "humm baby" Craig and GM Al Rosen.

Will Clark's first Major League swing results in a home run off Nolan Ryan on Opening Night at the Astrodome.

**1987:** Just two years after their 100-loss season, the Giants win the division thanks to late-season acquisitions of Kevin Mitchell, Dave Dravecky and Craig Lefferts from the Padres. They fall to the St. Louis Cardinals in the National League Championship in seven games. The Giants would take a 3-2 series lead back to St. Louis, but wouldn't score another run in the series after a four run fourth inning in their game 5 victory.

**1989:** On August 10, Dave Dravecky completes a miraculous recovery from surgery to remove a cancerous tumor from his pitching arm and defeats the Reds in front of a teary-eyed Candlestick Park crowd.

The Giants defeat the Chicago Cubs in the NLCS and face the Oakland A's in the first and only Bay Bridge World Series. On October 17, Game 3 is halted by a 7.1 earthquake at 5:04 pm. Play resumes 10 days later, and the Giants eventually get swept.

**1993:** Owner Bob Lurie, after failing in numerous attempts to get a downtown ballpark built, agrees to sell the team to a group that would relocate the franchise to the Tampa-St. Petersburg area. But a local investment group, led by

Peter Magowan, saves the franchise by buying the team on January 12 instead. Before the deal is even officially done, Magowan's group attracts superstar Barry Bonds to the squad.

**1996:** On April 27, Bonds becomes the fourth member of the prestigious 300-300 Club, launching his 300th and 301st home runs.

**1999:** The last home game of the 1999 season marks the last game the Giants play at Candlestick Park.

**2000:** The Giants christen Pacific Bell Park in inauspicious fashion, losing the first six games in the new yard and 11 of their first 15 games overall. Despite the slow start, the Giants went on to win the National League west with a 97-65 record, only to lose to the wild card and eventual National League champion New York Mets.

**2001:** With 39 homers at the All-Star break and three homers on September 9 to put him at 63, Barry Bonds goes on to bash 73 long balls that year to break Mark McGwire's record of 70.

**2002:** The Giants make it to the World Series for the first time since 1989 and were eight outs away from winning their first World Series since 1954. Taking a 5-0 lead into the 7th inning of game six, the Giants watched the Angels battle back to a 6-5 win and then defeat the shell-shocked Giants 4-1 in game 7.

**2007:** Barry Bonds eclipsed Major League Baseball›s all-time home run record, finishing with 762 clouts before retiring after the season.

**2008:** Pitching his first full season as a Giant, Tim Lincecum becomes the first Giant to win the Cy Young Award since Mike McCormick in 1967.

**2009:** Tim Lincecum became the first pitcher in history to win the Cy Young Award in each of his first two full Major League seasons.

**2010:** Catcher Buster Posey, the first Giant to be named National League Rookie of the Year since 1975.

With an 11-4 in the postseason against Atlanta, Philadelphia and Texas, the Giants win their first World Series since 1954 and, the first since moving to San Francisco in 1958.

**2012:** San Francisco finished 30-14 to run away with the National League West, before capturing its second World Series in three years, this time over the Detroit Tigers. They did so by winning six consecutive elimination games in the postseason, a feat only matched by the 1985 Kansas City Royals.

**2013:** A late-season surge prevented the Giants from becoming the only team besides the 1998 Marlins to finish in last place one year after capturing the World Series. The Giants delivered their finest offensive performance in a September 14 victory over Los Angeles when they scored 19 runs — the most ever tallied in a single game at Dodger Stadium.

**2014:** Only six games over .500 in mid-August, the Giants appeared to be in danger of making the postseason until a late season rally, fueled by a trade for pitcher Jake Peavy, the Giants snagged a wild card spot.

The Giants won a record 12 postseason games, including four against the Kansas City Royals, to win their third World Series title in six years. Madison Bumgarner burst into stardom to help San Francisco win its third World Series in five years. Madison Bumgarner excelled, yielding one run in 21 innings for a 0.43 ERA, and locked up Series Most Valuable Player honors by pitching a four-hit shutout in Game 5 before blanking the Royals for the final five innings on two days' rest in Game 7. Bumgarner was 2-0 with one save in the Series.

# SOURCES

*"Baseball Reference"*: https://www.baseball-reference.com/

*"Retro Sheet"*: https://www.retrosheet.org

*"MLB.com"*: https://www.mlb.com/giants/history

Alexander, Charles C. (1995). *Rogers Hornsby: A Biography.* New York City: Henry Holt and Company. ISBN 0-8050-2002-0.

D'Amore, Jonathan (2004). *Rogers Hornsby: a biography.* Westport, Connecticut: Greenwood Publishing Group. ISBN 978-0-313-32870-1.

# ABOUT THE AUTHOR

Jeff Wagner is a native of the Bay Area in California, and has been a fan of all Bay Area sports teams for over 50 years. This not only includes the San Jose Sharks and Golden State Warriors, but teams from both the San Francisco and Oakland sides of the bay: San Francisco 49ers/Giants and the Oakland Raiders/A's, something almost unheard of today!

Jeff attended his first Pro basketball game in 1966 (Warriors/Hawks), first NHL game in 1970 (Seals), first Pro baseball game in 1971 (Giants/Reds), and first Pro football game in 1976 (49ers/Saints). Jeff has attended numerous World Series, playoffs and All-Star games, including the 49ers/Dallas "The Catch" NFL Championship game in 1981.

Jeff has written several blogs on his experiences:
- Our Bay Area teams have been very good to us: http://drummer-jeff.blogspot.com/2012/10/our-bay-area-sport-teams-have-been-very.html
- My Top 10 Favorite Moments in Bay Area Sports History: https://drummerjeff.blogspot.com/2019/04/my-top-10-favorite-moments-in-bay-area.html
- My Top 10 Toughest Moments in Bay Area Sports History: https://drummerjeff.blogspot.com/2019/04/my-top-10-toughest-moments-in-bay-area.html

Jeff also likes playing the drums, and enjoys a blessed life with his wife Amy and their Pug Celia.

Other published books by Jeff:
Pug Shots: The Many Faces of a Chinese Pug:
*ISBN-10: 1481931865 | ISBN-13: 978-1481931861*